standard
grade
study-mate

english

standard
grade
study-mate

english

Walter Hayburn

Hamilton Publishing

standard
grade
study-mate

english

First Published 1990
© Walter Hayburn 1990
Reprinted 2000, 2004
ISBN 0 946164 21 5

All rights reserved. No part of this publication may be reproduced, stored in a retrieval system, or transmitted, in any form or by any means, electronic, mechanical, photocopying, recording or otherwise, without prior written permission from the publisher.

A catalogue record for this book is available from the British Library

**Visit Hamilton Publishing direct at
http://www.hamilton-publishing.com**

Orders can be made *direct* over the phone
Contact Thomson Litho, Hamilton Publishing (Sales)
on (01355) 233081

Mastercard and Visa Cards accepted

Letter accepted with school or personal cheque

The Author wishes to express his special thanks to the following people
Mrs Isabel Morrison; Mr John Mulligan; Miss Lynn Russell; and all pupils, past and present.

Published by
Hamilton Publishing
A division of M & A Thomson Litho Limited
10-16 Colvilles Place, Kelvin Industrial Estate,
EAST KILBRIDE G75 0SN

Printed and bound in Great Britain by
M & A Thomson Litho Ltd, East Kilbride, Scotland

INTRODUCTION

English! Who would imagine that something you use every single day could cause you such a problem? Yet here you are, preparing for your Standard Grade English exam, and suddenly you need help. Don't worry, because you're not alone. Of course, in class you can always find help: from classmates, or from your teacher. It's when you're trying to study alone that you will find this book most helpful.

This English Study-mate helps to take some of the strain out of studying, some of the torture out of tests, and some of the anxiety out of exams. Stage by easy stage, your Study-mate will show you what the Standard Grade English exam involves. It will let you in on some of the secrets about the exam papers' structure, and the types of questions you'll be asked. You'll be given advice on how to read for success and how to write with style.

You'll be shown examples of reading tests for the three different levels in Standard Grade: Foundation, General and Credit. These tests are to give you practice in tackling the different types of question you'll face in the exam. Most of the tests can be done in your own time; there's no hurry. It's more important that you learn *how* to do the tests than *how fast* you can do them. However, the last test at each level is designed to give you practice in working under exam conditions and must be done in fifty minutes, just like the real exam.

'That's all very well,' you might say, 'but how will I know how well I've done?' You'll find the answers to all the questions in each reading test in Chapter 7, so you'll be able to judge for yourself how well you're doing as you study. And if, as you're doing a test, you find yourself stuck at a question look no further than Chapter 4, where the study notes can give you a hint without giving you the answer. So, if you're finding one of the tests quite tough, rather than look up the answers right away, ask your Study-mate for a clue — a quick but careful read through the study notes to see if they can help. Because, of course, simply copying an answer isn't going to help you to improve your skills of reading.

The last test for each level will not have study notes. This is to allow you to use it like an actual exam paper. By doing it without the help of study notes, you will be able to see how you would do in the real thing! However, the answers for these last tests will be given, as well as a grade-score given for you to check your progress.

And there's more. You'll find the study notes helpful not only for the Reading tests, but for the Writing assignments, too. The Standard Grade English exams will test your writing skills as well as your reading skills. So in Chapter 6 you'll be shown four different types of writing question, each one presented in the same way as on the exam paper. The difference here is that you'll have the benefit of the advice given in Chapter 5, a little extra assistance from the study notes, and a writing routine to put your writing in good shape.

Don't worry: With your Study-mate, you can make the Grade!

WH

*This book is dedicated to the
late Mr James K. Scobbie,
my friend and former rector.*

GUIDE TO CONTENTS

· CHAPTER · ONE ·
ABOUT THE STANDARD GRADE ENGLISH COURSE
1

· CHAPTER · TWO ·
READING FOR TEST SUCCESS
3

· CHAPTER · THREE ·
READING TESTS

Foundation Level
Introductory Test	How the Cat Became	8–11
Test 2	The Gooseberry	12–14
Test 3	How to Complain	15–18
Test 4	Smith	19–25

General Level
Test 1	Scotland's Heritage	26–30
Test 2	Dracula	31–34
Test 3	Tartan Travels	35–38
Test 4	Elephants	39–40
Test 5	The Lost Boy	41–46

Credit Level
Test 1	The School Experience	47–49
Test 2	The Sweat Lodge	50–53
Test 3	Porphyria's Lover	54–56
Test 4	Great Expectations	57–59
Test 5	The Mouse	60–64

· CHAPTER · FOUR ·
STUDY NOTES ON READING TESTS

Foundation Level	Reading Tests	65–66
General Level	Reading Tests	66–68
Credit Level	Reading Tests	68–70

· CHAPTER · FIVE ·
'THE WRITE STUFF'
How to Tackle Writing Assignments
71

· CHAPTER · SIX ·
WRITING ASSIGNMENTS

Assignment 1	Conveying Information	75
Assignment 2	Arguing a Case	76
Assignment 3	Describing Personal Experience	77
Assignment 4	Writing a Short Story	78

· CHAPTER · SEVEN ·
ANSWERS TO READING TESTS

Foundation Level
Introductory Test	How the Cat Became	79
Test 2	The Gooseberry	79–80
Test 3	How to Complain	81
Test 4	Smith	82

General Level
Test 1	Scotland's Heritage	83–84
Test 2	Dracula	84–86
Test 3	Tartan Travels	86–87
Test 4	Elephants	87–88
Test 5	The Lost Boy	88–90

Credit Level
Test 1	The School Experience	90–92
Test 2	The Sweat Lodge	92–94
Test 3	Porphyria's Lover	94–97
Test 4	Great Expectations	97–98
Test 5	The Mouse	99–100

Acknowledgements
101

CHAPTER · ONE ·

ABOUT THE STANDARD GRADE ENGLISH COURSE

One of the major changes introduced by the Standard Grade course is that as well as the exam at the end, the work you do in class counts towards your overall grade. So maybe you should begin by finding out about the work you do *before* the exam, since it forms part of the assessment. Not only that, if you use the work in class to improve your English skills, you'll have less difficulty in passing the exam.

Basically, you do three kinds of work in Standard Grade English: reading, writing and talking. Although they appear to be separate, it is surprising just how much they have in common, and how much they help each other. For example, imagine you are asked to write about space travel. If you take some time to *read* about space travel, you will find that when it comes to *writing* about it, you have a lot more material for your essay. Reading helps writing. It's not just reading that helps. If you have to write about something like friendship, it's always a good idea to talk over your ideas with someone before you write. Talking can allow you to test out your own ideas and perhaps hear a few new ones. Alternatively, people in the discussion might ask you some questions that remind you of important facts you'd forgotten about or that make you set your thoughts in order. These are only a few ways that the three main English activities of reading, writing and talking help each other. There are others; for example, writing out rough notes to help you in making a speech, or reading a poem in order to find quotations to use in a talk. Can you think of any more?

The Standard Grade course lasts for two years, beginning at the start of third year. It sounds like a long time, but the work you do isn't just to prepare you for the exam at the end of fourth year. If that was all, it might be rather a waste of time. Believe me, it isn't wasted work!

FOLIO OF CLASSWORK

Much of your time during the course will be scripts, the reviews and reports, the poems, arguments and opinions, the personal experiences and diary entries, the character sketches and instructions, all of these things can be used to make up your *Folio of Classwork*. Folio of Classwork! Sounds pretty important: it is. It's an envelope to be sent by your school to the Scottish Qualifications Authority containing your five best pieces of classwork in Reading and Writing.

Three of the pieces in your Folio of Classwork should be Reading pieces. That is, pieces of writing that are directly about material you have read, at home or in class, during the two years of the Standard Grade course. For example, they can be character studies, or reviews of poems, plays, novels or short stories. Each of the three Reading pieces should be about a different text. Also, each should be about a different *type* of text. That means you can have a piece on poetry or drama or prose (novel or short story). If one of these doesn't suit you, you can replace it with a piece on Media Studies, that is, a piece written about for example a film, TV programme, or radio programme or programmes.

As well as three Reading pieces, you'll need two pieces of Writing work. It's only two because you'll be asked to do a third piece in the actual exam. The two you do in class will probably be better because you'll have longer to do each of them, and you should also be given an opportunity to make improvements to them. Be sure to take it! The two Writing pieces that go into your Folio should be different types of writing.

▶ **WRITING PIECE 1** *Choose either*
　　　　　　　　　　　a *or* **b**

a a piece of writing to convey information. It might be something as simple as a recipe or instructions for making a journey, or it could be as complicated as explaining how to go about a tricky hobby like fishing or hang-gliding.

b a piece of writing giving your thoughts

example, a real favourite with teachers is: Discuss whether it is right or wrong to carry out experiments on animals if the results help to save human lives.

▶ **WRITING PIECE 2** *Choose either* **a** *or* **b**

a a piece of writing in which you describe an experience, giving your thoughts and feelings about it. For example: Try to remember a time when you fell out with a close friend. Explain how this happened, what the result was, and describe your feelings at the time.

b a piece of writing in a particular form. For example, a short story, a poem, a script or a newspaper article.

If you have any doubts about what to put in your Folio, ask your teacher for advice. Your teacher will help when the time comes to make up the final version of the Folio of Classwork.

There you are, then: five pieces in the Folio of Classwork. These are sent off in fourth year, at the end of March, to the Scottish Qualifications Authority headquarters. If you work well in the class you will read a wide variety of texts and you'll be able to experiment with several different kinds of writing pieces. This will give you the best possible choice when it is time to decide on your five final choices for the Folio. You'll have the luxury of choosing only the best.

TALKING IN CLASS

All the work that gives you a Talking grade is completed in class and that amounts to one third of your overall grade. The Talking work is assessed by your teacher, who sends that mark to the Scottish Qualifications Authority which awards the Standard Grade certificates. So you can see how important talking (of the proper sort!) in class can be. Next time you're in a discussion group, or talking over a subject with a partner, or telling the rest of the class what you think, remember that your teacher is listening too! Your talking means marks.

Working hard at talking is very important because the Talking grade is worth so much of the final overall grade. It is also important for another reason: if you use Talking assignments carefully, they'll help to improve your reading and writing. As you've seen, the skills of reading, writing and talking overlap. So, in discussions, remember to listen to what others have to say about your ideas, and about their own ideas. When you're doing the talking, try out new words and technical terms, think of supporting reasons for the things you say, and try to explain clearly what you mean.

When you have to give talks to the rest of the class, use the opportunity to develop skills of research. Look for information on the subject of your talk: ask people who know a bit about it; find some books — ones you think can help you — and pick out some important ideas; use your own experiences, if possible. In other words, do a bit of detective work. When you find out more, you become more interested in a subject. All your detective skills can be used for Writing and Reading work, too.

...AND THEN THE EXAM

'Fine!' you say. 'But the exam! I hate exams. I'm not very good, and I don't know what they're all about!' Well, the rest of the book is going to tell you about the exam, show you what to expect, help you to prepare for it and show you the best ways of dealing with it. Don't worry: you can make the grade!

CHAPTER · TWO
READING FOR TEST SUCCESS

Exams make most people nervous—and Standard Grade Reading tests are no exception! Nerves *before* exams are normal. Nerves *during* an exam can mean disaster. Before an exam, a little bit of nervousness can help to keep your brain alert and ready to perform. It's like a runner making sure muscles are warmed up before the race begins. But during an exam, nerves upset your rhythm, they cloud your judgement, and spoil your concentration.

So, in the Reading test, as in any exam, you need a settled routine that shows nerves the exit. You need a routine so thorough and sure that nerves won't affect it. Not only that, you need a routine that produces results.

Some people in the Reading test like to begin writing their answers as soon as possible. They believe that the 'routine' of writing immediately chases away their nerves. Maybe it does—but a quick-write routine in a Reading exam is a formula for failure. *Don't do it!*

Pause for a minute. Think: what is a Reading test supposed to be testing? Your *reading* abilities! It's not really about writing at all. For some of the questions, you don't even need to write your answers in sentences. As long as your answer is clear and to the point, careless spelling won't lose you marks. A Reading test wants you to show by your answers that you've read the passage well enough to understand *what* the writer has written, and *how* it has been written.

This means that the amount of writing you need to do in a Reading test should not take any longer than twenty out of the fifty minutes the exam allows. The remaining half an hour is the time you use for reading and checking.

What do you read?

- the instructions and advice given on the front page (that way you shouldn't do the wrong thing *and* you'll learn something about the passage and what to look for)
- the passage (more than once, of course)
- the questions (*very* carefully)

How do you read?

That's the secret! An effective reading method for test success is vital. You must be able to

- what type of writing is being used as the test passage

This tells you:
- what the writer's aims and techniques are likely to be

This tells you:
- the way the passage has been written
- what the passage is about
- what main points the questions are likely to look at

ACTIVE READING

If you want to read for test success, there is a certain method of reading you should practise. Skimming over the passage quickly, as if you were looking for an address in your diary, or a phone number in the telephone directory, won't do.

You must read actively. That means that you should become involved in the passage—as you read, you analyse, you work out what is being said. Active readers ask questions all the time they read: Why did the writer begin at this point?—What difference does it make adding that phrase or missing out that word?—Why does this idea follow that one?—What does the writer feel about the subject? There are many more questions you might think of yourself.

One way to help you begin to ask these questions—a way of training you to read actively—is to miss words out of a passage. This will force you to ask yourself what the missing words might be. Another way is to mix up the order of the paragraphs. Then you will need to read each one and decide (by asking questions) where each paragraph should go.

You will notice that the first test in this book uses both techniques—missing out words and jumbling the order of paragraphs. This is to give you a chance to try Active Reading right away.

After that, you should try to practise the techniques for yourself. Here's how to do it. Ask a friend to find a piece of writing (it needs to be one you don't know) and to blank out some of the words. If you also find a passage for your friend, jumble the paragraphs—or if you

for yourself by filling in blanks and ordering paragraphs.

The more you practise exercises like these, the better your Active Reading skills will become. You'll discover that you understand more as you read. This is because you have become more involved in the reading, and are concentrating more on what has been written. Then, when you come to answer the questions, it should be easier because you will have understood more of what you read.

READING TEST TECHNIQUE

Active Reading, though, is only one part of the test success secret. You also need a straightforward and efficient test technique. This is a way of tackling tests in a careful, precise and successful fashion.

One very good way of dealing with Standard Grade English Reading tests is a double-reading method. You'll notice right at the start of all Standard Grade Reading tests that the instructions advise you to read the passage twice. This advice comes from the examiners themselves, so it's wise to take it seriously.

However, reading the passage twice is all very well, but what method of reading should you use, and what should each reading achieve? Here's what to do:

▶ READING No. 1

The point of the first reading is to give you a *general idea* of the test passage. You'll want to know what the passage is about, what type of writing it is, what the main points of the passage are and whether the writer is trying to make a case for a particular point of view or not.

The first thing you should do, then, is look at what the examination instructions have to say about the passage. These instructions usually introduce the passage and let you know what it is going to be about. They might even tell you particular things to look for when you're reading.

Next, pay close attention to the heading or title of the passage—if a heading or title is given. This should provide another clue as to what the writer's subject will be.

The last thing you give attention to during this first reading is the main point of each paragraph. Try to notice especially the first and last statements of each paragraph. At the beginning or end of every paragraph, the statements tend to introduce or sum up what the paragraph is about. Look for the main idea in these statements. A good way to do this is to try to think of a suitable title for each paragraph, one that has to do with the main point the paragraph is making. Extra attention at openings and endings, and thinking of titles for paragraphs, will help you to build up a clearer picture of the whole passage.

After your first reading check your time and if you have plenty of time in hand it might help you to read through the questions quickly. You *should not* answer them at this stage. The reason for looking at the questions is to find out what the examiner thinks are the important areas of the passage, and the main points the questions concentrate on. Are the examiner's main points the same as yours? If there is something the examiner asks about and you hadn't noticed it during your first reading, the second reading will give you a chance to make up for missing it first time around. Not only that, reading the questions might give you a clearer idea of what the passage is like. Very often, a question will contain a statement about what the writer is doing, and give you a line reference. Make use of such ideas from the questions to build up your understanding of the test passage.

▶ READING No. 2

The first reading and your look at the questions should have given you a general idea of what the passage is about and what the main point of each paragraph is. The second reading of the passage should take longer than the first one. The point of the second reading is to give you a chance to concentrate on the smaller but important details in the passage. These details will tell you not only the main ideas, they will also give you an understanding of the writer's use of evidence and description, of explanation and of matters of writing style.

Every word in the passage has been chosen deliberately, nothing is written by accident. In each passage, certain words or expressions are signals that particular directions are being followed. These words and expressions might be called *signposts*. One of your jobs during the detailed second reading is to *seek out the signposts*.

What do the signposts do?

> Signposts let you know when the writer is changing direction.

Here is a sentence with a signpost word, 'but': 'Many people love cats but just as many others prefer dogs'. The writer changed from writing about cat-lovers to people who prefer dogs. Other signposts that tell you a change in direction is happening include 'however', 'yet', 'nevertheless', 'although', 'on the other hand'.

☞ **Signposts tell you when an argument is being developed.**

Arguments, or discussions, are usually broken up by a good writer into several stages. As you read through a passage, you will be able to tell that a case is being made if the writer includes signpost expressions like 'first of all', 'secondly', 'finally', 'thus'. These signposts mark the different stages of the argument.

☞ **Signposts also tell you what stage you have reached in the writer's argument, discussion or description.**

'First', 'then', 'furthermore', 'to sum up', 'to conclude', 'not only...but also', 'as well as', are all signposts that you might find in this type of writing.

Can you find such phrases in an argument? Find a piece of writing that discusses an issue and look for the signposts in it.

☞ **Signposts tell you how valuable or important the writer thinks an idea or piece of information is.**

The writer will use several different kinds of material to make up the piece of writing. Some of the ideas or information will be more important than others. The writer lets you know an idea's importance by using signpost expressions like 'most importantly', 'an essential point', 'an idea worth noting', 'to a lesser extent', 'crucially', 'one basic piece of information', 'of major significance', 'above all', 'not so vital'.

☞ **Signposts tell you about the writer's confidence in opinions or facts.**

The writer's confidence will vary during a passage. Some ideas or opinions will seem very clear to the writer, and you will be able to tell this from the signpost words that are included. For example, 'It is *without doubt* the most enjoyable film I've seen'. Here, the writer is very sure, and the signpost tells you this. Other signposts like this include 'certainly', 'undoubtedly', 'without hesitation', 'clearly'.

On the other hand, a writer may include opinions that are less sure. If a writer is not so confident or certain about facts, you will notice different signposts from the ones above. The signposts of uncertainty include 'maybe', 'perhaps', 'it might well be', 'it may be true', 'possibly'.

So, looking carefully for the signposts makes what each signpost is pointing towards: is it a change of direction, a place in an argument or description, could the signpost be a clue to confidence, or a measure of importance?

However, your reading isn't finished at signposts. You also have to pay attention to points where an explanation or an example is given. Explanations and examples are there to make the main idea more obvious to the reader. If you were struggling during the first reading to see what the main idea of a paragraph was, finding explanations and examples in the second reading will be very helpful.

The last part of your second reading is to pick out unusual features of the author's writing, the features of style. Be on the watch for different types of language appearing in the same passage: language full of emotion; language that tries to persuade you; language that is highly descriptive; use of direct speech; changes of tone (maybe from formal to informal language); expressions of sadness or joy, anger or fear.

Do you see any figures of speech—metaphors or similes, or other expressions that make the writing more colourful, and easier to picture?

The second reading lets you decide on what effects the writer is trying to make on the person who is reading the passage. You are thinking about your reactions to the writer's style, about *how* something is written.

To give you a better idea, take a look at the two short descriptions below:

The Cat

The cat was black. It lay beside the fire with its eyes closed. It enjoyed the heat.

The Cat

The cat was as black as a midnight sky. It was stretched in slumber by the dancing flames, easy and dreaming in the warm glow.

What are the differences between these descriptions? What effect does each have as you read it?

Clearly, the second description has more stylistic features. These do not appear by accident, they are there for a reason. By using them the author hopes to control the way you picture what is being described. In other words, the choice of style is a deliberate attempt to influence the reader, and to manipulate the reader's reactions. The second reading should include looking for ways in which the writer tries to do this.

Each time you notice a feature of style (any

does the writer expect me to react to this? How could it have been written differently, and in what way is this feature special?'

> *What to do in reading two*
> *Is seek out signs and note key lines,*
> *Find examples and explanations*
> *To give you clear interpretations,*
> *And keep your eyes peeled all the while*
> *To note the writer's writing style.*

ANSWERING THE QUESTIONS

By using the double-reading method already described, you will have a good chance of building up a very clear idea in your mind of how each passage has been put together. You're now ready to answer the questions. Here are a few important points to keep in mind about your answers:

▶ Answer only what the question asks. Don't give extra information and don't forget key information. Too much or too little in an answer loses marks.

▶ Answer clearly. Always try to make your meaning obvious; a marker doesn't have the time to waste trying to unscramble your ideas, so be as exact as possible in your answers.

▶ If the question says 'use your own words', then avoid lifting whole chunks out the passage. Watch out for the phrase 'use your own words'.

▶ Fill in an answer to every question. No writing means no marks. If you don't know the answer, leave the question until the end. Then, if you still can't work it out, put down a guess *but only as a last resort*. It's better than nothing, but worse than trying to think it out.

▶ Don't waste too much time on a single question. Because your time is limited, you can't afford to spend it all on a question worth fewer marks than the questions you could move on to and answer.

▶ Unless you are asked, don't bother writing in sentences. It's a Reading test, not a writing one. You needn't repeat the words of the question. If asked 'Why did Jack and Jill go up the hill?' don't answer 'Jack and Jill went up the hill to fetch a pail of water.' All that writing wastes valuable time. Your answer should be brief but clear: 'To fetch a pail of water'.

▶ Always read over your answers carefully. Check that they answer the questions, that they are clear, that they refer to the correct parts of the passage. If the answers to two questions are the same — one is wrong because you can't expect two sets of marks for one answer!

CHECK YOUR READING RATING

Here is a list of questions which will help you to check your reading ability. Ask yourself the questions, answering each with one of the following: **always, often, sometimes, never**. Use the list regularly to check how your reading ability is developing.

1 Can you tell if the writer is arguing / describing / informing / telling a story / giving a personal experience?

2 Can you tell what the main point of an argument is (ie what the writer wants you to accept)?

3 Can you tell the difference between fact and fiction?

4 Can you tell the difference between opinion and fact?

5 Can you tell the writer's attitude to the subject of the passage (eg is the writer sincere, sarcastic, angry, delighted?)?

6 Can you pick out the topic of every paragraph?

7 Can you decide what a writer hints at rather than states directly? (ie can you read between the lines?)

8 Can you identify contrasts / parallels between ideas or people being described in a passage?

9 Can you see the different stages of a paragraph (eg statement, expansion / explanation, evidence / example, conclusion)?

10 Can you find and identify figures of speech and the effects they have on the reader?

11 Can you notice when there is a change of language / register / tone?

12 Do you check everything you have written?

THE PURPOSE OF THE READING TESTS

The Reading tests in the exams are designed to see if you can read in a particular way. The examiners for Standard Grade English have identified five main skills and the questions they set in Reading tests cover these five areas.

Skill a: Gaining an overall impression of the passage

Questions that test this skill will be trying to find out whether or not you've understood the general idea of the passage. In other words, they will test general responses such as: Do you know the main subject? What type of writing is it? What is your reaction to what is written? Why do you react that way?

Skill b: Obtaining particular information from the passage

Here, your ability to pick out particular facts and key pieces of information is being tested. For example, it may be important to notice how many people are mentioned in the passage, what time an event took place, what advice the writer is giving. Questions will ask you to look carefully for such information.

Skill c: Grasping ideas or feelings suggested by the passage

No piece of writing used in a Reading test is completely straightforward. There will be ideas and feelings that are not stated directly, yet these same ideas or feelings will be there. They'll be hinted at, or suggested, rather than clearly expressed.

You know the idea. Some friends give you a present. You don't like it. They ask 'Do you like it?' and, not wanting to offend them, but not wanting to lie either, you reply 'I've never been given anything like it!'. You haven't answered in a straightforward way that you like it. So there is a suggestion in your reply that you don't like it. Your friends grasp the feeling suggested although not stated directly, and offer to exchange it!

Skill d: Evaluating the writer's attitudes, assumptions, argument

This is more complicated. Not only do you need to work out what the writer is saying, but you have also to measure it against your own experience. Really what you're doing is using skills a, b and c, and adding to them the skill of judgement. Ask yourself the following questions: Do you think the writer's attitude is correct? Do you believe the writer should assume what he or she does assume? Do you agree with the case the writer presents? You'll be asked to explain your judgement.

Skill e: Appreciating the writer's craft

This skill demonstrates how aware you are of the effects of the writer's style on the reader. You are looking for ways the writer has used to express the meaning.

When you check your answers to the tests, you'll see that each question is testing one or more of these reading skills a, b, c, d, or e.

CHAPTER·THREE·
READING TESTS

Now it's time to try out some of the kinds of questions you will be facing in the Reading part of the Standard Grade exam. Good luck, and remember: *read actively* and *answer well*.

If you find yourself stuck at a question, try the study notes in Chapter 4. These may give you the hint that you need.

Once you've finished a test you can check your answers against those given in Chapter 7. You will notice that in all tests except the Foundation Level Introductory one, each question is allocated a range of possible marks, the maximum possible mark of 2 down to the minimum of 0. You must give a correct answer for each mark. For some questions you will notice that the marks jump from the maximum to the minimum with no intermediate marks. This means that to gain marks for one of these questions you must supply *all* the necessary information, not just part of it. The marks for all questions are shown as one of these two types: either 2/1/0 or 2/0. This is the way in which your answers will be marked in the exam.

The last test at each level, Foundation (Test 4), General (Test 5) and Credit (Test 5), is set out in a similar way to an exam paper and does not have study notes. Try to do each of these tests in fifty minutes, to make the test as much like the actual exam as possible. At the end of the answers section for each of these tests is an indication of what level of award you would have achieved if the tests had been your Standard Grade exam papers.

FOUNDATION LEVEL INTRODUCTORY TEST
How The Cat Became
Ted Hughes

Read the following test carefully. The passages are taken from a short story called *How The Cat Became* by Ted Hughes.

The test is divided into sections:

▶ **SECTION 1** is intended to assess your skills with *words* and *sentences*.

▶ **SECTION 2** is intended to assess your skills with *paragraphs*.

▶ **SECTION 3** is intended to assess your skills in understanding *a whole passage*.

Only once you have read through *all* the material of a Section should you begin to answer the questions that follow it. It is not always necessary to answer in sentences. Use your own words if the question asks you to do so. There are no study notes in Chapter 4 for this passage as all possible help has been included within the text.

▶ **SECTION 1** Read the following passage carefully, then answer the questions about it. Note that some words have been missed out of the passage on purpose.

Things were running very smoothly and most of the creatures were highly pleased with themselves. Lion was already famous. Even the little shrews and moles and spiders were .... well known.
But among all these busy creatures there was one who seemed to be getting nowhere. It was Cat.
Cat was a real oddity. The others didn't know what to make of him at all.
He lived in a hollow tree in the wood. Every night, when the rest of the creatures were sound asleep, he .... to the depths of his tree — then such

sounds, such screeching, yowlings, wailings! The bats that slept upside-down all day long in the hollows of the tree branches awoke with a start and fled with their wing-tips stuffed into their ears. It seemed to them that Cat was having the worst .... ever — ten at a time.

But no. Cat was tuning his violin.

If only you could have seen him! Curled in the warm smooth hollow of his tree, gazing up through the hole at the top of the trunk, smiling at the stars, winking at the moon — his violin .... under his chin. Ah, Cat was a happy one.

And all night long he sat there composing his tunes.

Now the creatures didn't like this at all. They saw no use in his music, it made no food, it built no nest, it didn't even keep him warm. And the way Cat lounged around all day, sleeping in the sun, was just more than they could stand.

'He's a bad example,' said Beaver, 'he never does a stroke of work! What if our .... think they can live as idly as he does?'

'It's time,' said Weasel, 'that Cat had a job like everybody else in the world.'

▶SECTION 1 QUESTIONS

1 *Five* words have been missed out of the passage. Without these words the sentences don't make sense. Think of a word to fit in each space so that the meaning of the sentence becomes clear, and write it down. Use your own words. **5/0**

2 In the table below you will see the meanings of words used in the passage. Try to find the words used in the passage that fit the meanings and write them down. Only *one word* from the passage fits each meaning. One word has been found for you to give you an idea of what to do. **5/0**

	Meaning	Word from Passage
	well-known, with a wide reputation	famous
(i)	something unusual and hard to understand	
(ii)	a short, shocked movement	
(iii)	writing, putting together	
(iv)	lazily passed the time	
(v)	with no thought of work or exercise	

▶**SECTION 2** This passage continues from the passage used in Section 1. However, the order of the paragraphs has been mixed up. Only paragraphs *a, b* and *c* have been kept in their correct order.

a So the creatures of the wood formed a Committee to persuade Cat to take a job.

b Jay, Magpie, and Parrot went along at dawn and sat in the topmost twigs of Cat's old tree. As soon as Cat poked his head out, they all began together, 'You've to get a job. Get a job! Get a job.'

c That was only the beginning of it. All day long, everywhere he went, those birds were at him, 'Get a job! Get a job!'

Other creatures that were about their daily work in the undergrowth looked up when Cat ran past. No one had ever seen Cat run before.

That night he went back to his tree early. He was far too tired to practise on his violin and fell fast asleep in a few minutes. Next morning, when he poked his head out of the tree at first light, the three birds of the Committee were there again, loud as ever, 'Get a job!'

He tucked his violin under his arm and suddenly jumped out at the top of the tree and set off through the woods at a run. Behind him, shouting and calling, came Jay, Magpie, and Parrot.

Cat ducked back down into his tree and began to think. He wasn't going to start grubbing around in the wet woods all day, as they wanted him to. Oh no. He wouldn't have any time to play his violin if he did that. There was only one thing to do and he did it.

And try as he would, Cat could not get a wink of sleep.

▶ **SECTION 2   QUESTIONS**

1 Read the paragraphs carefully and decide on the best order. When you have done so, note down the first few words of each paragraph in the order you think they ought to be in. For example, paragraphs *a, b* and *c* are given below.

paragraph a: 'So the creatures ...'
paragraph b: 'Jay, Magpie and Parrot ...'
paragraph c: 'That was only ...'
Complete the answer by writing down the first few words of paragraphs *d* to *i*.   **6/0**

2 Every paragraph contains *one* main idea. Look at the two longest paragraphs carefully. Write down the *main idea* of each of those two paragraphs using your own words.   **2/0, 2/0**

▶ **SECTION 3**   Read the following section very carefully before answering the questions.

a   Deer, Wild Boar, Bear, Ferret, Mongoose, Porcupine, and a cloud of birds set off after Cat to see where he was going.

b   After a great deal of running they came to the edge of the forest. There they stopped. As they peered through the leaves they looked sideways at each other and trembled. Ahead of them, across an open field covered with haycocks, was Man's farm.

c   But Cat wasn't afraid. He went straight on, over the field, and up to Man's door. He raised his paw and banged as hard as he could in the middle of the door.

d   Man was so surprised to see Cat that at first he just stood, eyes wide, mouth open. No creatures ever dared to come on to his fields, let alone knock at his door. Cat spoke first.

e   'I've come for a job,' he said.

f   'A job?' asked Man, hardly able to believe his ears.

g   'Work,' said Cat. 'I want to earn my living.'

h   Man looked him up and down, then saw his long claws.

i   'You look as if you'd make a fine rat-catcher,' said Man.

j   Cat was surprised to hear that. He wondered what it was about him that made him look like a rat-catcher. Still, he wasn't going to miss the chance of a job. So he stuck out his chest and said, 'Been doing it for years.'

k   'Well then, I've a job for you,' said Man. 'My farm's swarming with rats and mice. They're in my hay stacks, they're in my corn sacks, and they're all over the pantry.'

l   So before Cat knew where he was, he had been signed on as Rat-and-Mouse-Catcher. His pay was milk, and meat, and a place at the fireside. He slept all day and worked all night.

m   At first he had a terrible time. The rats pulled his tail, the mice nipped his ears. They climbed on to rafters above him and dropped down — thump! on to him in the dark. They teased the life out of him.

n   But Cat was a quick learner. At the end of the week he could lay out a dozen rats and twice as many mice within half an hour. If he'd gone on laying them out all night there would pretty soon have been none left, and Cat would have been out of a job. So he just caught a few each night — in the first ten minutes or so. Then he retired into the barn and played his violin till morning. This was just the job he had been looking for.

▶ SECTION 3   QUESTIONS

1 Is this story fiction or non-fiction? Give a reason for your answer.   **2/1/0**

2 a What interesting word is used in the passage to describe a gathering of birds?   **2/0**
   b Why do you think it was a good word to use?   **2/0**

3 Look again at paragraphs *a*, *b* and *c*. What is it about Cat that makes him different from the other animals? Give a possible reason for this difference   **2/1/0**

Look at paragraphs *d–i*. They will help you to answer the next two questions.

4 What is it about Man's appearance that tells you he was surprised to find Cat at his door?   **2/0**

5 What reason did Man have for thinking Cat would be good at catching rats?   **2/0**

6 Why do you think Cat sticks out his chest in paragraph *j*?   **2/0**

7 There are several statements below about the passage. Some are true, some are false. Write down the number at the beginning of each statement and put T beside it if you think it is true, or F beside it if you think it is false.

   (i)   The farmer didn't really need Cat's help; he just felt sorry for Cat
   (ii) Cat was a very experienced rat-catcher
   (iii) Cat found the job on Man's farm easy from the very start
   (iv) Cat was very pleased with his new job   **2/1/0**

8 What skill helped Cat most during his first week on the farm?   **2/0**

9 What do you think Cat's violin *really* was?   **2/0**

10 In your opinion, what would the other creatures say if they could see Cat working on the farm?   **2/0**

FOUNDATION LEVEL TEST 2
The Gooseberry
Joan Lingard

Using the double-read method described in Chapter 2, read the following passage before going on to answer the questions. It is taken from a novel by Joan Lingard called *The Gooseberry*. This novel is about a young girl called Ellen and how she comes to terms with her mother marrying Herbert, her mother's second husband and not Ellen's real father.

If you are finding the passage difficult, take a look at the study notes in Chapter 4.

1   Herbert did not waken till nine that Sunday morning. It was unusual for him to sleep so late but he had been restless during the night (he had eaten a tomato sandwich for supper) and at one point had wakened thinking the house was being burgled only to realise that he must have been dreaming. He pulled on his dressing-gown and went through to the kitchen to put on the kettle. He always made Rose a cup of tea on weekend mornings.

2   The morning was bright and sunny and two of his yellow roses were beginning to unfold. He wanted to go out and look at them close up. Should he nip out in his dressing-gown? Would the neighbours see? Well, what if they did? The thought came, surprising him. He tied his dressing-gown cord more firmly around his middle and made to unlock the back door. It was not locked. He frowned. He was sure he could remember locking it last night; he had never once forgotten, not even on the night his mother died. The lock was unlocked and the snib also drawn back. He opened the door and peered out gingerly as if he half expected a burglar might be lurking round the corner. The people two doors down had had their bungalow turned inside out three months back; it had made everyone on the street very cautious since. There was no one in the garden. He remembered again the faint noises in the night. Quickly he closed, locked and snibbed the door.

3   'Rose,' he called, going back to the bedroom, 'don't panic but I think we've been burgled.'

4   Rose shot out of bed at once, reaching for her housecoat. 'What have they taken?'

5   'I don't know yet. I've just found the back door open. They must have come in through a window.'

6   They went to the sitting room. It was dim and shrouded, the curtains were drawn just as they had left them last night. On pulling them back they saw that the windows were tightly shut, their snibs undisturbed. There were only two other windows a burglar could have come in by: the bathroom, if he was thin, and Ellen's, if he was not. The bathroom window proved untouched.

7   Herbert followed his wife to Ellen's room almost falling over her heels. She stopped in the doorway, her hand to her mouth.

8   'What is it, love?'

9   'Ellen's gone.' Her reaction was overdramatic, she realised that at once, and changed it to, 'She's not in her bed.'

10   Herbert gave a sigh of relief. That explained the opened back door. Ellen must have gone for an early morning walk. Rose nodded but did not look too convinced. Somehow it was not like Ellen although she would be the first to admit that one never could know what Ellen might get up to.

11   'Let's go and have our tea,' said Herbert.

12

12   On their way to the kitchen they saw the envelope standing on the ledge below the picture of Herbert's mother. The letter was addressed to 'Mrs H. Hall'.

13   'Mrs Hall,' she read. 'How strange! It looks like Ellen's handwriting.'

14   The writing was indeed Ellen's. Her mother had to sit down on a stool in the kitchen to read it and Herbert had to put three spoonfuls of sugar in her tea to help counteract the shock.

15   'She's run away! Oh, Herbert, what are we going to do?'

▶ QUESTIONS

1 Once you have read the whole passage carefully, write down a suitable title for it.   **2/0**

2 Look again at paragraph 1.
   a You are told that Herbert had slept longer than usual. Below is a list of possible reasons for this. Write down the one you think is the best reason.
      Herbert had slept longer than usual:
      A because he always did that on a Sunday
      B because he had really been enjoying his sleep
      C because he had had a disturbed night
      D because tomato sandwiches for supper always made him sleep longer   **2/0**
   b Write down the single word from paragraph 1 that helped you to answer question 2a.   **2/0**

3 This question is about Herbert's hobby and habits. It will help if you read paragraphs 1 and 2 again, and then look at the two definitions below:
   Hobby: favourite occupation or interest that is not a person's main job.
   Habit: a normal or regular way of behaving, a routine.
      In paragraphs 1 and 2, you read about a hobby Herbert enjoys, and about three of Herbert's habits. Find his hobby and three of his habits that are mentioned and write them down.
      Herbert's hobby   **2/0**
      Three of Herbert's habits   **2/1/0**

4 Paragraphs 1 and 2 also help you to decide what kind of character Herbert is. Below are some words which might describe Herbert:

   lazy   careful   careless
   angry   happy   timid

   a Choose the *three* words that describe Herbert best and write them down.   **2/1/0**
   b Why did you choose these three words? Give a reason from the passage to explain each of your choices.   **2/0, 2/0, 2/0**

5 In paragraph 3 Herbert tells Rose not to panic.
   a Does she take his advice? Answer *yes* or *no*.   **2/0**
   b What *two* words from the passage helped you decide on an answer for 5a?   **2/0**

6 Read over paragraphs 5 and 6 again.
   a What is Herbert's reason for thinking the house has been burgled?   **2/0**
   b How does Herbert believe the burglars entered the house?   **2/0**
   c What information from earlier in the passage supports Herbert's belief that the house has been burgled?   **2/0**

7 Paragraph 7 tells you that Herbert followed Rose to Ellen's room, and that he was 'almost falling over her heels'. Why do you think Herbert was following so closely?   **2/0**

8 Read over paragraphs 7, 8 and 9 again. These paragraphs describe how Rose reacts when she finds Ellen is not in her room.
   a Name two things that Rose does when she first discovers Ellen is not in her room.   **2/1/0**
   b Why is Rose's reaction said to be 'overdramatic'?   **2/1/0**
   c In your own words, explain the difference between the phrases 'Ellen's gone', and 'She's not in her bed' as they are used in paragraph 9.   **2/1/0**

b What does he now think has happened? **2/0**

c Do you think Rose agrees with her husband at this point? Answer *yes* or *no*. Give a reason for your answer. **2/1/0**

d In what way does Herbert try to calm his wife? **2/0**

10 In paragraph 12, Rose and Herbert discover a letter. Even before she opens it, Rose describes the letter as 'strange' (paragraph 13). Why should Rose say this before she knows what is inside? **2/1/0**

11 Opposite is a diagram of Herbert and Rose's house. You will notice that only the hall, and the back and front door are shown. Copy the diagram and draw in all the other rooms you think there are in the house, in the places you think they should go. **1** mark for each correct room marked.

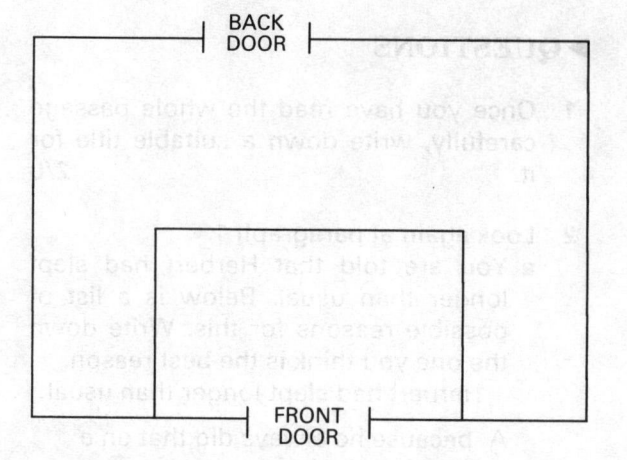

FOUNDATION LEVEL TEST 3
How to Complain
The Association for Consumer Research

Use the double-read method to read the following passage before going on to answer the questions. It is taken from a booklet explaining how to make complaints about faulty items.

If you are finding the passage difficult, take a look at the study notes in Chapter 4.

▶ SECTION A   COMPLAINTS ABOUT GOODS

1 A typical example: you buy a cassette tape in a sale. A week later the tape breaks, and cannot be played. What should you do?
2 It is best to take it back to the shop as soon as the problem occurs. If this is not easy, perhaps because you live a long way off, write to say you are dissatisfied with the product and ask for collection arrangements to be made. Any unexplained or unreasonable delay in doing this will weaken your case.
3 Many people believe that the first complaint about faulty goods should be made to the manufacturers. This is *not* the case. Your contract is with the retailers, the party who sold you the goods. It is to the retailers that your complaint should be made.

▶ SECTION B   HOW TO COMPLAIN

Make your complaint to the right person

1 It is always a good idea to ask for the manager in a shop or the departmental manager in a large store. In asking for a person in authority you also show that you mean business right from the start.
2 Don't be fobbed off with the common response that the manager is 'in a meeting' or 'away'. Insist that someone must have been left in charge and that you'll see that person. Failing that, register your complaint with the assistant and make an appointment to call back and see the manager at a mutually covenient time.
3 If you do agree to call back on another occasion you may be asked to leave the goods so that the manager has time to inspect them. This is not wholly unreasonable on the shop's part, but as a general guideline try to avoid leaving goods behind. If you decide to leave the goods with the shop, make sure you get a receipt and ask them to write on it 'for inspection only'. This may prevent a dispute

Be polite but firm

4 When making your complaint it is important that you adopt the right tone. The last thing you want to do is deliberately antagonise the person you are dealing with. You should try to be polite but firm and to give a generally businesslike impression. Maintain this approach and avoid having a row.

Know what you want

5 It is remarkable how many people return faulty products to the seller not having the faintest idea what they want to happen. Do you want a full refund, a repair, a credit note or an exchange? You may not get what you want but you should decide beforehand.

Take a receipt

6 Wherever possible try to take your receipt back with the goods. A receipt can prove that the goods were bought from a particular shop or store. A shop will want to make sure that the goods were bought there before considering your complaint. However, you are not legally obliged to show a receipt. You may have some other proof of purchase: for example, you may have a cheque stub or credit card voucher, or a particular trader's name may be stitched or stamped on to the product, or an assistant may remember you, or you may have had someone with you when you bought the goods.

▶SECTION C   KNOW THE LAW

1 Knowing your legal rights can give you confidence and put you in a stronger bargaining position. Every time you buy goods, even second-hand goods, from a shop, mail order catalogue, indeed from any business, you enter into a contract with the seller. Under this contract the law places upon both parties a number of obligations. The most important obligations that the seller owes you, the buyer, are laid down in the Sale of Goods Act 1979. The obligations are:

- that the **seller owns the goods**
- that the **goods correspond with any description given**
- that the **goods are of merchantable quality**
- that the **goods are fit for their purpose.**

Description

2 If any description is applied to the goods, part of the contract is that the goods will match that description. For example, if the colour or size of an item is specified on its box the item must be of that colour or size. Otherwise the seller will be in breach of contract and you can insist on a refund — if you act quickly.

Merchantable quality

3 Being of merchantable quality means that the goods will be fit to do the job that you would reasonably expect of goods of that type, taking into account their price, age and so on. So a washing machine must wash, food be fit to be eaten and shoes fit to be worn, regardless of whether or not they were bought in a sale. If goods are not of merchantable quality, the seller will have broken his part of the contract and is obliged to compensate you. If you act quickly you will be entitled to a refund. If a reasonable time has elapsed and you have thereby accepted the goods in the legal sense you are entitled to claim the cost of repair. If the goods cannot be mended, you can claim the difference in the value of the goods as they should have been and the goods as they are.

4   The supplier is also obliged to compensate the customer for any loss suffered as a result of the product's defect. For example, if a faulty tumble dryer damages a number of items of clothing the customer will be entitled to compensation for any reasonable loss suffered as a result of the fault, as well as a full refund of the purchase price of the tumble dryer.

Fitness for purpose

5   If you bought an item for a specific purpose, made that purpose known to the seller and then acted on his recommendation, this too is part of your contract — that the goods will be fit for the purpose you made known. For example, if you seek the advice of an assistant in a hardware shop about the type of glue to stick wood together and he recommends a particular one, then if the glue does not in practice do the job the seller is in breach of contract and you are entitled to compensation.

6   All these rights apply provided the goods were bought from a business. If they were bought privately, for instance through the small ads column of a local newspaper or from a neighbour, the goods do not have to be of merchantable quality or fit for their purpose but they still have to be as they are described.

▶ SECTION A QUESTIONS

1   At the end of paragraph 1, the writer asks 'What should you do?'
In your own words, write down the *two* possible things to do.   **2/1/0**

2   a Who should you complain to first if goods are faulty, the makers or the sellers? Choose one and write it down.   **2/0**
    b From the passage, give a reason for your answer to **2a**.   **2/0**

3   The word 'contract' is a word to do with the law. It is a technical term. Can you give another example of a technical term from Section A?   **2/1/0**

▶ SECTION B QUESTIONS

4   If you look at the letters in Section B, you will notice that three different kinds of letters are used. These are: heavy capital letters, heavy letters, and ordinary letters. What is each kind of letter used for? Complete the sentences below. The first is done to show you.
Heavy capital letters are used *to headline the subject of Section B.*
Heavy letters are used ...

5   a According to the writer, who is the 'right person' to listen to your complaint?   **2/0**
    b Give a reason from the passage for complaining to this person.   **2/0**

6   This passage tries to offer as much advice as possible to help you if you have to make a complaint.
    a In the case of complaining to the right person, what *two* excuses given by the shop should you not accept? Write them both down.   **2/1/0**
    b If these two excuses are used, write down the *two* best courses of action you can take.   **2/1/0**

7   Below are some possible meanings of the word 'allegation' (Section B, paragraph 2). Write down the meaning you think fits best.

complaint	claim
promise	threat **2/0**

8   a According to the writer, why is it important that you 'adopt the right tone' (Section B, paragraph 4) when you are making a complaint?   **2/1/0**
    b Give two ways mentioned in the passage that help you to 'adopt the right

9 Look again at Section B, paragraph 5.
   a Is the writer surprised that many people return faulty goods but don't know what they want in return? Answer *yes* or *no*. **2/0**
   b Write down the word from paragraph 5 that helps you to answer question **9a**. **2/0**
   c Here is a list of things that might happen when you return faulty goods. Write down the letters of the *four* which, according to the writer, would be the best solutions to the problem.

   A You should have the chance to buy a new item
   B You should start a violent argument with the manager
   C You should be told that the manager is not in to help you
   D You should be given all your money back
   E You should have a friendly chat with the shop assistant
   F You should have the item repaired
   G You should have the chance to take a different item of the same value
   H You should be given the same type of item as a replacement **2/1/0**

10 Look over Section B, paragraph 6 once more. How many ways are given of proving that you bought goods from a particular shop? Write down *one* of the following:
   1, 3, 4, 6, 8. **2/0**

▶ SECTION C   QUESTIONS

Section C is carefully organised. First, it mentions the law and the four main points from the *Sale of Goods Act* 1979. Next, it explains three of the main points in more detail.

11 Which main point is *not* explained in more detail? Suggest a reason for this. **2/1/0**

12 Read Section C, paragraph 4 once again. It contains a rule from the *Sale of Goods Act* 1979. Now, use this rule to solve the following example:
   A man buys a microwave oven for £200. He puts a chicken costing £5 in it to cook. The microwave is faulty, and blows up the chicken. How much should the man claim from the shop? Choose one of the following and write it down: £200, £195, £250, £205. **2/0**

13 Do you think this passage helps you to understand how to complain? Give a reason for your answer. **2/1/0**

14 Below are three statements taken from the whole passage. Some statements are *facts,* some statements are *opinions*. For each statement, put F if you think it is a *fact,* or O if you think it is an *opinion*.

   (i) Your contract is with the retailer (Section A paragraph 3)
   (ii) The last thing you want to do is deliberately antagonise the person you are dealing with (Section B, paragraph 4)
   (iii) If you act quickly you will be entitled to a refund (Section C, paragraph 3) **2/1/0**

FOUNDATION LEVEL TEST 4
Smith
Leon Garfield

This passage is taken from a novel called *Smith* by Leon Garfield. The test appears as it would in the Standard Grade exam. Try to complete it in no more than fifty minutes. There are no study notes. You can use this test to check how well you are progressing in your reading development.

Spaces have been left for the answers to show you how the exam paper will look. In the exam you will write your answers in the spaces provided, or you may be asked to tick a box or underline a word on your answer paper. *If this book belongs to your school please do not write in it. Ask your teacher what to do.*

This 'paper' would assess Grades 5 and 6 for a Standard Grade Foundation Level award.

Read the following passage carefully. It is from a book which tells about the adventures of a young boy called Smith.

When you have read it — and it will help if you read it through twice — you should go on to answer the questions.

Try to answer all the questions.

1   Footsteps. The door opened. Two footmen with real hangmen's faces. Alarm seized Smith. Why had they come? And why so grim?
2   'Up with you!' said one.
3   'And then down with you!' said the other.
4   'W-what d'you mean?'
5   They grinned. 'Miss's instructions. She says, afore you commence on scrubbing the yard, that self-same necessary thing must be done to you! So down to the scullery, young Smith!'
6   Smith's eyes glittered in alarm. Most likely he paled, too ... but it wasn't so easy to see. He looked about him. But there was no escape. He looked up at the footmen. No mercy, nor even pity, there.
7   'To the scullery, young Smith.'
8   Now Smith had never been washed since, most likely, the midwife had obliged, twelve darkening years ago. Consequently, he suspected the task would be long, hard and painful. He was not mistaken.
9   Two more footmen, aproned over their livery, stood ready and waiting by a steaming iron tub.
10 'Take off them wretched rags, Smith.'
11 'Rags? What rags?' (The scullery was grey and stony and full of strong vapours).
12 'Your clothes, Smith. Take off your clothes.'
13 The window was barred and the door was shut. He began to undress. Disdainfully, the footmen watched him; and indignantly, he stared back.
14 'Ain't you never seen a Person take off his clothes before?'
15 Disdain gave way to amusement ... and then to surprise. Several times the footmen reached forward to seize him, for they thought he'd finished, but each time he waved them back.
16 ''Ave the goodness to wait till I'm done, gen'lemen! 'Ave the goodness!'

anyone's knowledge, he'd never thrown a single item away. Coats and waistcoats worn to nothing but armlets and thread now came off him, and shirts down to wisps of mournful lace: one by one, removed carefully and with dignity, then dropped, gossamer-like, to the floor.

18   Then there were breeches consisting of nothing more than the ghosts of buttonholes, and breeches that came off in greasy strips – like over-cured slices of ham; and breeches underneath that were no more than a memory of worsted, printed on his lean, sharp bottom.

19   These memories of perished clothes were everywhere, and plainest of all on his chest, where there was so exact an imprint of ancient linen that Smith himself was deceived – and made to take off his skin!

20   At last he crouched, naked as a charred twig, quivering and twitching as if the air was full of tickling feathers.

21   'Ready,' he said, in a low, uneasy voice, and the four footmen set to work. Two held him in the tub; one scrubbed, and one acted as ladle-man. This task was on account of the water having been dosed with sulphur, and consisted in spooning off Smith's livestock as it rushed to the surface in a speckled throng.

22   From beginning to end, the washing of Smith took close upon three hours, with the scullery so filled with sulphurous steam that the footmen's misted faces grew red as the copper saucepans that hung like midnight suns on the scullery's streaming walls.

23   At last it was done. He was taken out, rinsed, and wrapped in a sheet – the ghost of his former self. For he was now a stark white replica of the previous Smith and, had his sisters seen him they'd have shrieked and sworn it was his spectral image!

24   His clothes were burned before his oddly saddened eyes ... which eyes were now seen to be somewhat larger and rounder than might have been supposed. But his hair, in spite of the shock and scrubbing, remained as black as the river at night.

25   'Me clothes', he said. 'Me belongings. I can't go about like this.'

QUESTIONS

1 Why was Smith seized with *alarm* even before the footmen spoke?

2 What do the footmen say has to be done to Smith?

3 Write down the phrase from paragraphs 5–7 that tells you Smith was a prisoner.

4   How old is Smith?

   _____

5   What do you think 'livery' (paragraph 9) means?
    Tick (✓) the answer you think is correct.

    | All the buttons on a waistcoat | |
    | Shoes worn by a servant | |
    | A type of uniform | |
    | A bath | |
    | Strong-smelling soap | |

6   Look again at paragraphs 1–7.
    a   Where in the house do you think Smith is being held prisoner?
        Tick (✓) the answer you think is correct.

        | Somewhere in the cellar | |
        | Somewhere out in the yard of the house | |
        | Somewhere in the attic | |

    b   Write down the word or phrase from paragraphs 1–7 that helped you to answer **6a**.

        _____

7   In paragraph 14, Smith says 'Ain't you never seen a Person take off his clothes before?'
    This is not correct English.

    a   Write Smith's sentence again, but put it into correct English.

        _____

        _____

b Why do you think the writer has made Smith use incorrect English? Tick (✓) the answer which you think is correct.

Because the writer didn't know any better	
Because Smith was in a terrible temper	
Because it makes Smith's speech more realistic	
Because Smith enjoyed making mistakes	

8 Here is a list of words or phrases that *might* describe how the footmen felt as they watched Smith undress.
From what you have read in the passage, tick (✓) the *three* boxes that describe the footmen's feelings.

very sad ☐   ready to laugh ☐   amazement ☐
anger ☐   disgust ☐   disdain ☐

9 Look again at paragraphs 17–18.
a What reason is given for Smith wearing so many clothes?
_____
_____

b Write down the words from this section which tell us that Smith's clothes might smell badly.
_____

10 Later in the passage, when Smith is being washed, there is evidence that Smith had a definite problem connected with being so dirty.

a What proof of this problem is mentioned in the passage?
_____

b Why do you think Smith was in this condition?
_____
_____

11 Look at these two pieces taken from the passage. They are both about Smith. *Underline* the word or phrase from the list beneath each which best describes Smith at that moment.

   a 'At last he crouched, naked as a charred twig, quivering and twitching as if the air was full of tickling feathers'.

      READY TO LAUGH   BITTERLY COLD   IN A LOT OF PAIN

            VERY FRAGILE   VERY NERVOUS

   b 'He was taken out, rinsed, and wrapped in a sheet — the ghost of his former self. For he was now a stark white replica of the previous Smith ...'

      TERRIFIED   A PHANTOM   BLEACHED

          WASHED CLEAN   WHITE WITH COLD

12 Look once more at the section where Smith is being washed.
   a What are the *three* tasks being done by the footmen?

      (i) _____

      (ii) _____

      (iii) _____

   b What words that describe the footmen suggest that washing Smith was a difficult job?

      _____

      _____

13 Look again at paragraph 24.
   a Why do you think Smith's clothes were burned?

      _____

      _____

   b How did Smith feel about this? Explain in your own words.

      _____

      _____

14 Here is a list of things that *might* describe Smith.
From what you have read in the passage, tick the *three* boxes that describe Smith.

| thin ☐ | very bad-tempered ☐ | not at ease ☐ |
| age 14 ☐ | dark haired ☐ | well built ☐ |

15 a Which of the answers below do you think gives the time when this story takes place?
Tick (√) the answer you think is correct

The present day	
About twenty years ago	
About forty years ago	
About a hundred years ago	

b Choose a word or a phrase from the passage that helped you to decide.

_____

16 a Which of the following would make the best title for the whole passage?
Tick (√) the best one.

The Prisoner	
The Footmen and Smith	
Smith is Given a Bath	
The Scullery	
How to Bath a Boy	

b Give a reason for your choice.

_____

_____

17 This passage is taken from a book called *Smith*.
Tick (√) *one* of the following statements which you think best describes what is most likely to happen next.

a The footmen push Smith into the yard without his clothes. Dressed in only a towel, he is forced to clean the yard for four hours. ☐

or

b Smith kicks one of the footmen on the shins and makes a run for the door. He escapes as far as the street but a policeman, seeing a boy in a towel, stops him and takes him back to the house. The footmen punish him for trying to escape.

or

c The footmen take Smith, still dressed only in a towel, back to the room where he started and leave him there.

or

d The sisters of Smith come for him. They don't recognise him now that he is clean so they leave without him.

or

e The lady of the house asks to see Smith. The footmen give him new, clean clothes for him to meet her. She is very kind and says she will give him a job.

18 a Now that you have read the complete passage, do you think Smith was fortunate or unfortunate to be in the house?

Tick (√) your answer.

FORTUNATE ☐   UNFORTUNATE ☐

b Give a reason for your answer.

_____

_____

[*END OF QUESTION PAPER*]

GENERAL LEVEL TEST 1
Scotland's Heritage
National Trust for Scotland and *Historic Scotland*

This test is based on two pamphlets. Read them carefully using the double-read method. The aim of each pamphlet is to encourage the public to take out membership of an organisation interested in Scottish history. If in difficulty, don't forget the study notes in Chapter 4.

The questions are divided into *three* sections:

▶ **SECTION 1** asks only about the *Historic Scotland* pamphlet, on page 27.

▶ **SECTION 2** asks only about the *National Trust for Scotland* pamphlet, on pages 28 and 29.

▶ **SECTION 3** asks about *both* pamphlets.

Only after you have read through all the material should you begin to answer the questions.

▶ SECTION 1 QUESTIONS

All the questions in this section are about the *Historic Scotland* pamphlet only (page 27).

1 Who sponsors the Historic Scotland organisation? **2/0**

2 Why does the writer use so many commas in Block 1? **2/0**

3 The table below contains several statements about Fort George. Only *one* statement is completely correct. Choose the statement you think is completely correct and write down its letter, A, B, C or D. **2/0**

A Fort George is an 18th-century fort within fifteen miles of Inverness. It was built before the village of Ardersier existed and before the battle of Culloden took place.

B Fort George lies to the west and north of Ardersier and less than ten miles from Culloden. It was built in Inverness.

C Fort George is an 18th-century fort over ten miles north and east of Inverness. It lies close to the village of Ardersier.

D The building of Fort George began after the battle of Culloden. It is more than a dozen miles from Inverness and is a 19th-century fort.

Now look again at Block 2. The next two questions are about what Block 2 contains.

4 In your own words, state the *main task* carried out by the Historic Scotland organisation. **2/1/0**

5 Block 2 tells you about both the past and the future. Below are some words used in Block 2: some are about the past, others are about the future. Write them down. Beside each word or phrase write P if you think it is about the past or F if you think it is about the future. The first two are done to give you an example. **2/1/0**

3000 BC — P

future visitors — F

historic —

preserve —

Battle of Culloden —

throughout the centuries —

time honoured —

6 Look now at Blocks 2, 3 and 4.
   a The list below contains some definitions of the phrase 'time honoured stones'. Write down the letter of the definition you think is correct. **2/0**

   'time honoured stones' means:

   A stones that have been ignored except by a chosen few.

   B boulders worn down by the feet of unfriendly visitors.

   C buildings that have an historic importance.

   D areas of rock with great geological value.

(Continued on page 29 – second column)

BLOCK 1

WE'VE BEEN *visited by* THE SCOTS, *the* PICTS, THE ROMANS, *the* SAXONS, THE *NORMANS*, *the* VIKINGS, *& the* ENGLISH.

BLOCK 2

FORT GEORGE
11 miles NE of Inverness, by the village of Ardersier. Begun in 1748 following the battle of Culloden.

Historic Scotland has 330 properties from Skara Brae on Orkney to Jedburgh Abbey in the Borders.

Some dating back to 3000 BC. Throughout the centuries, these time honoured stones haven't been short of visitors, though on occasion, friendship was sadly lacking.

To preserve our castles, palaces, gardens and abbeys for future visitors, we need friends.

Friends, who will visit and cherish them.

For as little as £10 each year you can become a Friend of the Scottish Monuments. (A family ticket is only £15, senior citizens £5.)

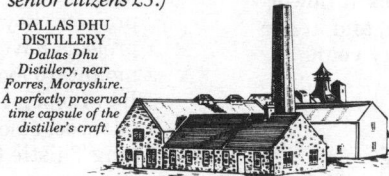

DALLAS DHU DISTILLERY
Dallas Dhu Distillery, near Forres, Morayshire. A perfectly preserved time capsule of the distiller's craft.

BLOCK 3

JEDBURGH ABBEY
Founded by David I dating from c. 1118, perhaps the finest of the four great Border Abbeys.

MANY *HAVE become* OUR LIFELONG FRIENDS.

HISTORIC SCOTLAND
Historic Scotland, 20 Brandon Street, Edinburgh EH3 5RA.
Tel: 031-244 3099. (Monday-Friday 9am-5pm)

Supported and Sponsored by
gateway

BLOCK 4

STIRLING CASTLE
Dominates the surrounding areas from its 250ft rock and once housed Wallace, Bruce, Mary Queen of Scots.

For this sum, you'll have a full year's free entry to all our sites and, in your first year, half price entry to English Heritage and Welsh Cadw sites too. Free entry in your second year.

There's a free Directory packed with information and maps plus a regular newsletter to keep you in touch with all our activities. Special site visits for Friends are guided by our professional staff. Life membership brings you all these benefits for a single payment.

If you would like to become a Friend of the Scottish Monuments you will find an application form overleaf.

Nowadays, Scots, Picts, Romans, Saxons, Normans, Vikings and English are more than welcome to apply.

EDINBURGH CASTLE
Standing proudly on a rock that has been a fortress since time immemorial.

BLOCK 5

BECOME *one of our* FRIENDS

Please complete this form for the type of membership you require and send it with payment to Historic Buildings and Monuments, S.D.D., P.O. Box 157, Edinburgh EH3 5RA. Cheques should be made payable to "Scottish Office". Or use the attached Direct Debit form.

FULL NAME_____
(BLOCK LETTERS PLEASE)
ADDRESS_____
_____
_____POSTCODE_____

ANNUAL MEMBERSHIP
ADULT .... £10.00 ☐
FAMILY *(free entry for parents and children up to 16 yrs)* .... £15.00 ☐
REDUCED *(Senior citizens and young people in full-time education up to 21 years)* .... £5.00 ☐
SENIOR CITIZEN COUPLES
(Man and wife qualify for State Pension) .... £7.50 ☐

MEMBERSHIP FOR LIFE
SINGLE PERSON .... £140.00 ☐
JOINT LIFE *(For husband and wife. Each receives a membership card)* .... £220.00 ☐
SINGLE PERSON OAP .... £70.00 ☐
JOINT LIFE OAP *(For OAP couples. Each receives a membership card)* .... £110.00 ☐

METHODS OF PAYMENT
BY CHEQUE ☐   BY CREDIT CARD ☐
Access ☐ Visa ☐ American Express ☐
Card Number
Expiry Date

This brochure and the one overleaf were produced several years ago, so some details are now out of date. Historic Scotland and the National Trust for Scotland continue to conserve and promote Scotland's heritage, and to encourage the public

ALL THAT WE DO ◆ WE DO FOR YOU

Left: Culzean Castle after stonework restoration.

Below: Youth in Trust repairing sand-dune erosion on Iona.

a The National Trust for Scotland belongs to you – to the people who love Scotland – and opens its properties for the enjoyment of all.

b That's why the brooding magnificence of Glencoe, the soaring mountains of Kintail and the peaceful beaches of Iona are there for all to see and enjoy, protected for posterity.

c At Inverewe Garden, where palm trees grow on the same latitude as Labrador, or Brodick where the rhododendrons win prizes at flower shows on both sides of the Atlantic, and in our gardens throughout Scotland, thirty young gardeners are now being trained.

Above: Glencoe, the mountaineers' paradise.

d And at our Gardening School at Threave, we run a two-year residential course for the head gardeners of the future.

e At Culzean Castle, Robert Adam's masterpiece overlooking the Clyde, the stonework is eroded by time and needs continual restoration. Repairs to the viaduct, now in progress, will take a team of stonemasons several years to complete.

f And the contents of our properties require as much painstaking care and attention as the exteriors. We have our own bookbinding, metalwork, picture-framing and conservation

Below: Prize winning rhododendron at Brodick.

workshops, providing training for young people, the craftsmen of the future. And, unseen, we maintain craft skills of bygone years with the restoration of decorative plasterwork, pictures and even weathercocks.

g Youth in Trust volunteers help to conserve the landscape and wildlife at our properties by the projects they carry out all over Scotland. Recent projects have included weekends repairing mountain footpaths at Ben Lomond and Glencoe, also week-long Thistle Camps helping to maintain ancient woodlands at Drum and repairing eroding sand-dunes at Iona.

h But maintaining properties costs money. Gardens need re-planting, curtains frayed with age need to be repaired, and paths on mountains

Above: Restoring the binding of valuable books from the libraries of houses in the Trust's care.

Left: Razorbills at St Abb's Head National Nature Reserve.

Below: Restoring plasterwork at House of Dun.

worn by feet need re-seeding. We repair leaky roofs, antiquated plumbing and rusting suits of armour. The list is endless.

i Each year it costs us over £8 million to carry out this work, quite apart from any new projects we may wish to undertake. That's why we need your help as a member.

Benefits of Membership

We don't ask for much; we believe that we give so much in return. For example, the cost of a single membership for a twelve-month period is £15 and a whole family can join for £24.50, less than an average family night out. In exchange we give you:

① _____

Free Admission to over 100 properties in Scotland open to the public, plus over 300 properties of the National Trust, a completely separate organisation, in England, Wales and Northern Ireland.

② _____

Our quarterly coloured magazine, *Heritage Scotland*, with lists of events, winter activities and a host of opportunities for you to enjoy.

③ _____

Our annual, illustrated *Guide to Properties*, showing opening times and facilities available at them, together with our *Annual Report*.

④ _____

Priority booking for our holiday cottages, adventure base camps for groups, St Kilda Work Parties, Thistle Camps for young people and our Caravan Parks and Camp Sites.

⑤ _____

Details of our Cruises, guided walks and Ranger/Naturalist programmes. And for those who want to do a little more, details of how to join one of our Members' Support Groups.

⑥ _____

Facilities at our properties for all the family – grandparents, parents and children – including shops with our especially designed range of goods and tearooms when you need to take the weight off your feet.

Six good reasons for joining, but, most important of all, the Trust needs the help of people like you to support its work. So, if you care for your heritage, please come and join us as a member.

National Trust for Scotland

(Continued from page 26)

b Which 'time honoured stones' mentioned in the pamphlet have not been illustrated? **2/0**

7 Look at the list of items below. All are available from the Historic Scotland organisation. Write down the number of each item and state whether it is *free* or has to be *paid for*, eg (i) paid for

   (i) membership for a family of four
   (ii) a day at one of the English Heritage sites in the first year
   (iii) the directory of the Historic Scotland organisation
   (iv) entry to one of the Historic Scotland sites in the first year
   (v) the Historic Scotland organisation's newsletter
   (vi) entry to a Welsh Cadw site in the second year. **2/1/0**

8 Look now at Block 5. This question is based on what Block 5 tells you.

A number of people interested in joining the Historic Scotland organisation are described below. Decide how much the membership would cost for each one and write it down, eg (i) £10

People Interested in Becoming 'Friends of Scottish Monuments'

   (i) Ms A. Carnegie, 24 years old. Single. Enjoys climbing, drives a Porsche, works in banking. Doesn't smoke. One-year membership wanted.
   (ii) Mr and Mrs Gerontion. Husband, aged 72, worked in Post Office. Wife, 69, retired teacher. Both fit and active for age. Seek life membership.
   (iii) Mr Jim Scott. Studying at Cairnhill College. Enjoys outdoor life, smokes occasionally. Aged 19 years and 2 months. Single year's membership wanted.
   (iv) The Campbell family. Father, 46, runs a shop. Mother helps in shop at weekends. Daughter, Margaret (17) still at school. Son Denis in first year at same school. Want membership for one year. **2/1/0**

▶ **SECTION 2 QUESTIONS**

All the questions in this section are about the *National Trust for Scotland* pamphlet only.

9 Explain in your own words *two* ways that

10 Read paragraph *a* again. In your own words, what kind of person does the National Trust for Scotland want as a member? **2/0**

11 Pick out *two* single words in paragraph *b* that describe typical features of the Scottish landscape. **2/1/0**

12 This pamphlet mentions three areas in which the National Trust for Scotland is active: gardening, building and conserving the natural world. For each area of activity, give *one* location where that activity takes place and state what the project in that place is.

Area of Activity
(i) gardening **2/0**
(ii) building **2/0**
(iii) conserving/natural world **2/0**

13 Below are several statements. Say whether each statement is false (F) *or* true (T).

(i) The National Trust for Scotland wants to attract young members.
(ii) The stonework at Culzean Castle has been restored.
(iii) The National Trust for Scotland spends a total of £8 million per year. **2/1/0**

14 Find the two photographs, the first of Iona, the second of the House of Dun, and look at them carefully. In your own words, explain the difference between *restoring* as it is used to describe the work at the House of Dun, and *repairing* as it describes the work on Iona. **2/0**

15 'Unseen' is used in paragraph *f*, but not in its usual sense. What do you think it means as it is used in paragraph *f*? **2/0**

▶ SECTION 3 QUESTIONS

The questions in this section are about *both* pamphlets.

16 Both pamphlets contain a slogan, or catchphrase. These are short sentences to help the reader remember what each organisation is hoping to achieve.
  Write down the slogan or catchphrase for each organisation. **2/1/0**

17 Which organisation should you join if you wish to have *free* entry into the greatest number of places in Britain during your first year of membership? Write down evidence from both pamphlets to support your answer. **2/1/0**

18 The National Trust for Scotland feels that it doesn't ask for much money to become a member. What phrase from the Historic Scotland pamphlet tells you that it feels the same? **2/0**

19 a Historic Scotland, in Block 4 of its leaflet, says that membership lasts 'a full year'. Why do you think the word 'full' is used? **2/0**
  b What words does the National Trust for Scotland use which mean the same as 'a full year'? **2/0**

20 Each organisation offers *six* reasons for becoming a member. *Two* of the reasons for joining are the same for both organisations. Write down the two reasons that the organisations have in common, using your own words. **2/0**

21 Write down the name of the organisation which you think has the more interesting pamphlet. Why do you think this? **2/0**

GENERAL LEVEL TEST 2
Dracula
Bram Stoker

Use the double-read method to study the passage before attempting the questions. It is taken from the novel *Dracula* by Bram Stoker, which is about the famous vampire.

If you are finding the passage difficult, take a look at the study notes in Chapter 4.

1   *5 May.*—I must have been asleep, for certainly if I had been fully awake I must have noticed the approach to such a remarkable place. In the gloom the courtyard looked of considerable size, and as several dark ways led from it under great round arches it perhaps seemed bigger than it really is. I have not yet been able to see it by daylight.

2   When the calèche stopped the driver jumped down, and held out his hand to assist me to alight. Again I could not but notice his prodigious strength. His hand actually seemed like a steel vice that could have crushed mine if he had chosen. Then he took out my traps, and placed them on the ground beside me as I stood close to a great door, old and studded with large iron nails, and set in a projecting doorway of massive stone. I could see even in the dim light that the stone was massively carved, but that the carving had been much worn by time and weather. As I stood, the driver jumped again into his seat and shook the reins; the horses started forward, and trap and all disappeared down one of the dark openings.

3   I stood in silence where I was, for I did not know what to do. Of bell or knocker there was no sign; through these frowning walls and dark window openings it was not likely that my voice could penetrate. The time I waited seemed endless, and I felt doubts and fears crowding upon me. What sort of place had I come to, and among what kind of people? What sort of grim adventure was it on which I had embarked? Was this a customary incident in the life of a solicitor's clerk sent out to explain the purchase of a London estate to a foreigner? Solicitor's clerk! Mina would not like that. Solicitor — for just before leaving London I got word that my examination was successful; and I am now a full-blown solicitor! I began to rub my eyes and pinch myself to see if I were awake. It all seemed like a horrible nightmare to me, and I expected that I should suddenly awake, and find myself at home, with the dawn struggling in through the windows, as I had now and again felt in the morning after a day of overwork. But my flesh answered the pinching test, and my eyes were not to be deceived. I was indeed awake and among the Carpathians. All I could do now was to be patient, and to wait the coming of the morning.

4   Just as I had come to this conclusion I heard a heavy step approaching behind the great door, and saw through the chinks the gleam of a coming light. Then there was the sound of rattling chains and the clanking of massive bolts drawn back. A key was turned with the loud grating noise of long disuse, and the great door swung back.

5   Within, stood a tall old man, clean-shaven save for a long white moustache, and clad in black from head to foot, without a single speck of colour about him anywhere. He held in his hand an antique silver lamp, in which the flame burned without chimney or globe of any kind, throwing long, quivering shadows as it flickered in the draught of the open door. The old man motioned me in with his right hand with a courtly gesture, saying in excellent English, but with a strange

6 'Welcome to my house! Enter freely and of your own will!' He made no motion of stepping to meet me, but stood like a statue, as though his gesture of welcome had fixed him into stone. The instant, however, that I had stepped over the threshold, he moved impulsively forward, and holding out his hand grasped mine with a strength which made me wince, an effect which was not lessened by the fact that it seemed as cold as ice — more like the hand of a dead than a living man. Again he said:

7 'Welcome to my house. Come freely. Go safely. And leave something of the happiness you bring!' The strength of the handshake was so much akin to that which I had noticed in the driver, whose face I had not seen, that for a moment I doubted if it were not the same person to whom I was speaking; so, to make sure, I said interrogatively:

8 'Count Dracula?' He bowed in a courtly way as he replied:

9 'I am Dracula. And I bid you welcome, Mr Harker, to my house. Come in; the night air is chill, and you must need to eat and rest.' As he was speaking he put the lamp on a bracket on the wall, and stepping out, took my luggage; he had carried it in before I could forestall him. I protested, but he insisted:

10 'Nay, sir, you are my guest. It is late, and my people are not available. Let me see to your comfort myself.' He insisted on carrying my traps along the passage, and then up a great winding stair, and along another great passage, on whose stone floor our steps rang heavily. At the end of this he threw open a heavy door, and I rejoiced to see within a well-lit room in which a table was spread for supper, and on whose mighty hearth a great fire of logs flamed and flared.

11 The light and warmth and the Count's courteous welcome seemed to have dissipated all my doubts and fears. Having then reached my normal state, I discovered that I was half-famished with hunger.

12 My host, who stood on one side of the great fireplace, leaning against the stone-work, made a graceful wave of his hand to the table, and said:

13 'I pray you, be seated and sup how you please. You will, I trust, excuse me that I do not join you; but I have dined already, and I do not sup.'

14 I had finished my supper, and by my host's desire had drawn up a chair by the fire and begun to smoke a cigar which he offered me, at the same time excusing himself that he did not smoke. I had an opportunity of observing him, and found him of a very marked physiognomy.

15 His face was a strong — a very strong — aquiline, with high bridge of the thin nose and peculiarly arched nostrils; with lofty domed forehead, and hair growing scantily round the temples, but profusely elsewhere. His eyebrows were very massive, almost meeting over the nose, and with bushy hair that seemed to curl in its own profusion. The mouth, so far as I could see it under the heavy moustache, was fixed and rather cruel-looking, with peculiarly sharp white teeth; these protruded over the lips, whose remarkable ruddiness showed astonishing vitality in a man of his years. For the rest, his ears were pale and at the tops extremely pointed; the chin was broad and strong, and the cheeks firm though thin. The general effect was one of extraordinary pallor.

16 Hitherto I had noticed the backs of his hands as they lay on his knees in the firelight, and they had seemed rather white and fine; but seeing them now close to me, I could not but notice that they were rather coarse — broad, with squat fingers. Strange to say, there were hairs in the centre of the palm. The nails were long and fine, and cut to a sharp point. As the Count leaned over me and his hands touched me, I could not repress a shudder. It may have been that his breath

was rank, but a horrible feeling of nausea came over me, which, do what I would, I could not conceal. The Count, evidently noticing it, drew back; and with a grim sort of smile, which showed more than he had yet done of his protuberant teeth, sat himself down again on his own side of the fireplace. We were both silent for a while; and as I looked towards the window I saw the first dim streak of the coming dawn. There seemed a strange stillness over everything; but as I listened I heard, as if from down below in the valley, the howling of many wolves. The Count's eyes gleamed, and he said:

17 'Listen to them — the children of the night. What music they make!' Seeing, I suppose, some expression in my face strange to him, he added:

18 'Ah, sir, you dwellers in the city cannot enter into the feelings of the hunter.' Then he rose and said:

19 'But you must be tired. Your bedroom is all ready, and tomorrow you shall sleep as late as you will. I have to be away till the afternoon; so sleep well and dream well!' and, with a courteous bow, he opened for me himself the door to the octagonal room, and I entered my bedroom...

Dracula

▶ QUESTIONS

1 The passage begins with a date, 5 May. From this, what form of writing might you expect? **2/0**

2 a What time of day did Jonathan Harker arrive? Write A, B or C.
   A early morning
   B mid-afternoon
   C late evening
   Write down the phrase from paragraph 1 which helps you to decide.
   2/1/0
  b At what kind of building do you think Jonathan has arrived? Give a reason for your answer. **2/0**

3 a In your opinion, what is a 'calèche' (paragraph 2)? **2/0**
  b Write down *one* feature of a calèche which is mentioned in the passage. **2/0**

4 Look again at paragraph 3.
   Jonathan has been left outside the building and he doesn't know what to do.
   a How does he feel at this moment? **2/0**
   b Give *three* possible reasons mentioned in paragraph 3 for his feelings. **2/1/0**
   c Why does the writer describe the walls as 'frowning' at the start of paragraph 3? **2/1/0**

5 We are told in paragraph 3 that Jonathan has come all the way from London to visit Dracula.
   a Where are we told that Dracula lives? 2/0
   b What does Jonathan do for a living? 2/0
   c In your own words, explain why Jonathan has come to visit Dracula. 2/0

6 a In paragraph 6, Dracula is described as if he were stone. Because he is like stone, he is similar to the place where he lives. Write down another *two* features that Dracula and his dwelling have in common. 2/1/0
   b It goes on to say that Dracula 'moved impulsively forward'. What does this tell you about how he was feeling? 2/0

7 a What *two* features of Dracula's handshake surprise Jonathan? 2/1/0
   b Why should these features be surprising? 2/1/0

8 a What doubt does Jonathan have in paragraph 7? 2/0
   b What *two* things make this doubt possible? 2/1/0

9 Read over paragraphs 8, 9, and 10 once more. List *three* things Dracula has done or does to make Jonathan feel welcome. 2/1/0

10 In your own words, say what the word 'dissipated' means (paragraph 11). What phrase from paragraph 11 helps you to answer this question? 2/1/0

11 Look carefully at paragraphs 5 and 15. On page 33 is a photograph of Dracula taken from a film. You will notice that it is different from the description in the passage in some ways, and that it is similar in others. There are at least *four* ways that it is different, and at least *five* ways it is similar. Make two lists; one should be headed 'Differences' and one 'Similarities'. Find the differences and similarities and put them under the correct heading. 2/1/0, 2/1/0

12 Look over paragraphs 16, 17 and 18 again.
   a What effect does Dracula have on Jonathan in paragraph 16 and what does this cause Jonathan to do? 2/1/0
   b Why does Jonathan believe he reacted in this way? 2/0
   c What single word used in paragraph 17 tells you that Dracula's attitude towards the howling of the wolves is unusual? 2/0

13 As Jonathan at last enters his bedroom, what do you think he is feeling about his arrival at Count Dracula's? 2/1/0

14 The writer wants to show how Jonathan's moods and feelings change. He does this by using *contrasts*. A contrast places two things together and shows how different they are. An example of a contrast in the passage is the contrast between the *darkness* in the courtyard (described in paragraphs 1, 2 and 3) and the *well-lit* room where Jonathan is taken for supper.
   In the table below is a list of features mentioned in the passage. Find the contrasting feature that the writer has used to make a contrast with each of the features listed in the first column of the table. The first is done for you as an example.

Feature	Contrasting Feature
Darkness of the courtyard	well-lit supper room
(i) Dracula's age	2/0
(ii) The silence of the courtyard	2/0
(iii) The warmth of the room	2/0
(iv) The warmth of Dracula's welcome	2/0

GENERAL LEVEL TEST 3
Tartan Travels
Walter Hayburn

Use the double-read method on the following passage, then attempt the questions which follow it. The passage is about a trip to the top of the highest mountain in Europe, and the return to the foot.

If you are in difficulty, you can always find help in the study notes on this passage which appear in Chapter 4.

1. Only a few years ago, I was travelling through Europe by car with my wife when Night told us it was time to stop. Well, I say Night told us, but actually it was my wife who told me it was time to stop. It just sounded more poetic and seemed more visual to say 'Night told us'. It made me sound less of a Jessie, too, of course.

2. Anyway, I digress. My wife was hungry and it was time to stop. And where we stopped, so it chanced, was at the foot of Mont Blanc, although as I said, it was night, and big and all as Mont Blanc is, you couldn't see it in the dark. It's an indisputable fact of life that even things the size of Mont Blanc are invisible in the dark.

3. Well, when we awoke in the morning (having dined beautifully and slept like Alpine logs) who should be waiting outside our hotel for us? Mont Blanc, of course. She hadn't budged all night—the mountain, that is, not my wife, who has a tendency to roll over in her sleep. 'Isn't it lovely?' she said—she being my wife, not the mountain.

4. I agreed.

5. 'So clean, so powerful,' said my wife.

6. I agreed.

7. 'So rugged and tall. So impressive,' continued my wife, and by now I had realised that she wasn't speaking about her husband, but about Mont Blanc.

8. I agreed, anyway, as was my wont.

9. 'We should go to the summit,' said my wife.

10. I ... would not wish you to think that I'm altogether a fool. I didn't agree immediately. Instead, I attempted to suggest that we were ill-equipped for such a venture. Very reasonably, I thought, I cast doubt on the availability of sherpas, before proceeding to ask whether my wife knew how to handle a llama or had considered what I understood to be the punitive costs of feeding a yak.

11. 'It's the highest mountain in Europe,' said my wife in that impervious way beloved of all wives when blissfully ignoring the earnest, and often eloquent, pleas of their husbands, whose wishes run counter to the determination of their better halves.

12. Anyway, I agreed — that is, that Mont Blanc is indeed the highest mountain in Europe, 'But,' I said, 'does that mean we are obliged to go to its summit?'

13. 'I want to go,' said my wife.

14. Now, I am very fond of my wife, and moreover, I could see that she was very enthusiastic, shall we say, about going to the top. (It was the gleam of battle in her eye that betrayed this enthusiasm, you see). Her one concession to my reluctance was an assurance that we would take the cable-car. A wise concession, I have to admit, since it rendered my sherpa/llama/yak gambit utterly useless.

while to sound casual. My wife quite correctly interpreted this as meaning that I was bothered—terribly—and that I didn't want to go.

16   However, some vestiges of machismo remained in my adulterated heart, and I didn't yet wish to reveal to my wife my dreadful fear of heights—a fear that had never revealed itself in all the years of our acquaintance. (I'd lived in a bungalow when we first met, you see).

17   So there I was, vainly—in both senses of vainly—trying to conceal my fear of heights from the newly-discovered Edmund Hillary who was alive and well and living in my wife.

18   'Great things are done when men and mountains meet,' said my wife.

19   I just stared, in silence, at my wife—could this really be my dear physics teacher?

20   'Blake,' she added, 'William,' and continued to smile sweetly in my direction. She was maddeningly in command of the situation, and even using my own province, English literature, to persuade me.

21   It's no good, I thought to myself, the game is up, the truth will out, no substitutes allowed!

22   'I'm a hero,' I assured her, 'with coward's legs: a hero from the waist up!'

23   This is my husband, she was thinking, the English teacher.

24   'Milligan,' I added, 'Spike,' and smiled my defeat, and braced myself for the ascent.

25   I had tried to muster enthusiasm for the idea and, inasmuch as enthusiasm can be defined as that point at which affection outweighs judgement, I succeeded. For let it be said, I love my wife and would deny her nothing.

26   We got to the cable-car at the foot of the mountain and I was agreeably surprised. The car was a fairly large affair, about the size of a bread van. My wife insisted that I wasn't to offer to test the cable before going on board, so we climbed straight in.

27   My first hint that all was not as I thought it should be came when I discovered there was no stewardess to strap me into my parachute, and to soothe any mounting fears as we moved up the mountain.

28   Worse was to follow and I became acutely aware of the accuracy of that definition of a human being as an ingenious assembly of portable plumbing. This occurred when we were to disembark from the bread-van about a third of the way up, and board a smaller cable car to continue the ascent. Now, where the first cable-car had no stewardess, this second one, I swear, would have made Dan Dare check his life insurance. But not the jolly, suicidal skiers who crammed into the mini-bus sized cabin with us. How much trust can you place in someone who fixes a bendy stick to the end of each leg and hurtles down the side of a mountain at high speed, dodging other folk on bendy sticks and yodelling until a collision occurs? Or let me put it another way — how much should a hero with coward's legs trust someone with a bendy stick attached to each foot etc etc? NOT A LOT.

29   And still the ordeal wasn't over. Two-thirds of the way up—all change again.

30   'Isn't the mountain grandly impressive, marvellously spectacular and what a view!' I said to my wife between clenched teeth, and trying to hide my white knuckles—mainly by biting my fingernails up to the wrist. 'How can you know that?' my wife asked, witheringly. 'Come out of the corner of the cable-car and let the man send it back down!'

31   The final leg of the ascent was made in what can only be described as a telephone booth. The only reassurance I could have derived from this would have been if Clark Kent had been changing in it at the time. He wasn't.

32   We made it to the top. The views were magnificent. My wife was pleased. But it's all downhill from here, if you'll pardon the pun.

33   The return in the phone booth was made in the company of two elderly Italian couples on holiday from Milan. Now, Italians are famed as a happy, friendly people. Elderly Italians from Milan, I live to assure you, are all of that—and lively, too. They meant to squeeze every ounce of fun from their trip, and who am I to grudge anyone fun? Don't say it—a hero with coward's legs.

34   We may have got off, these delinquent jovial Italian geriatrics and myself, to a bad start. Maybe I should have been more tolerant of their continental exuberance and their attempts at perverse Italian humour as the phone booth lurched sickeningly out of the terminus into the clear Alpine air, suspended only by a filigree thread of reinforced steel cable WHICH I WAS NOT ALLOWED TO CHECK! But I must say that I thought their shouts of 'WHEEEEE, Milano, andiamo!' which, translated, means 'Wheee, Milan here we come!', were in extremely bad taste.

35   However, we struck up conversation—how can six folk in a telephone booth avoid it?—and, in my feeble Italian (a sample of which you have been given already) I told one of the old gentlemen that my wife and I were from Scotland.

36   'What's that? said the old man's wife—except she spoke in Italian, of course.

37   'Scozia!' said her husband.

38   'Where?'

39   'Scozia!' Celtic! Rangers! Motherwell!' he said.

40   The message, though, wasn't getting through to the poor old woman. It seemed my suspicions that women everywhere know little or nothing of football—not even Motherwell—had been confirmed.

41   However, there is one thing that most folk notice about Italians. They are very expressive with their hands. Desmond Morris calls it Body Language. I call it psychopathic idiocy.

42   Nothing loth, the old fellow decided to demonstrate my wife's and my origins to his wife in actions. For his wife, he put on the Edinburgh Military Tattoo in a phone booth that was swinging thousands of feet above *terra firma*. He was the massed pipe bands of the Royal Scots Guards, the Cameronians and the Highland Light Infantry, marching, playing imaginary bagpipes, and ululating in a demented Milanese impersonation of the pipes while simultaneously attempting to impress by the actions of his free hand (he was playing the pipes one handed!) that he was wearing a skirt. Only a skirt, mind you, because, even in the sophisticated body language of the Italians, tartan is hard to do in actions — especially if you're playing the bagpipes.

43   Tartan Travels? Well, sort of.

►QUESTIONS

1 a Below is a list of words that appear in the passage. In your own words, give the meaning of each word as it is used by the writer.

   (i) indisputable (paragraph 2)   **2/0**
   (ii) wont (paragraph 8)   **2/0**
   (iii) concession (paragraph 14)   **2/0**
   (iv) muster (paragraph 25)   **2/0**

word from the passage to fit each of the meanings below.

   (i) having the wish to destroy oneself (paragraph 28)
   (ii) scornfully, not admiringly (paragraphs 29–31)
   (iii) liveliness (paragraphs 33–35)
   (iv) wailing, howling (paragraph 42)

2 What *three* reasons does the writer give for saying 'Night told us' (paragraph 1)? Explain in your own words. **2/1/0**

3 a The writer repeats the phrase 'I agreed' three times (paragraphs 4–8). In what way does the writer use this repetition to affect the way you think of his character? **2/0**

b What else does the writer say about himself which adds to the impression of his character? Give two examples. **2/0**

4 a The writer claims to act 'very reasonably' in the questions he asks (paragraph 10). Do you agree? Give a reason for you answer. **2/1/0**

b What *two* reasons does the writer have for asking his wife such questions? **2/1/0**

c Is his wife worried by the questions? Quote from the passage to support your answer. **2/1/0**

5 a In paragraph 14, the writer asks if you will accept the word 'enthusiastic' to describe his wife. What phrase in the same paragraph tells you that 'enthusiastic' is not the best word to use? **2/0**

b Why should the writer decide to use 'enthusiastic'? Suggest a better, more appropriate word. **2/1/0**

6 a What emerges as the real reason for the writer not wishing to go to the top of the mountain? **2/0**

b The writer says that his wife did not know about this reason. In your own words, explain why this should be so. **2/1/0**

c What *are* the two senses of the word 'vainly' (paragraph 17) as it is used in the passage? **2/1/0**

7 Explain in your own words what is unusual about the phrase 'smiled my defeat' (paragraph 24). **2/1/0**

8 Paragraph 27 gives an example of comic exaggeration.
a What is being exaggerated? **2/0**
b Explain this exaggeration. **2/1/0**

9 What is the writer's attitude to the skiers (paragraph 28)? Quote *briefly* from the passage to support your answer. **2/1/0**

10 A pun (paragraph 32) is a comic way of giving one word two meanings at the same time.
a What word is made into a pun? **2/0**
b Give both possible meanings as used in the passage. **2/1/0**

11 What football team does the writer support? Give a single word in the passage which tells you this. **2/1/0**

12 a Why do you think the writer gives the passage the title 'Tartan Travels'? **2/1/0**

b Why does he end with the phrase 'Well, sort of,'? **2/0**

GENERAL LEVEL TEST 4
Elephants
Guy Lefrançois

Using the double-read method, read the following passage which is about elephants. It is taken from a book called *Psychology* by Guy Lefrançois. Go on to answer the questions.

If you are having difficulty, take a look at the study notes in Chapter 4.

1. Common people have two types of memory: like elephants or like sieves. It has long been thought that the former offers certain very definite advantages over the latter. Sadly, however, the legend has been found to be mythical. Elephants have lousy memories!

2. Still, elephants are fascinating creatures. They are the largest land mammals on this planet, and are considerably older than the human species — almost 60 million years older. At one time there were more than three hundred species of these huge beasts; now there are two.

3. It was long thought that the elephant was a creature of singular intelligence, endowed with grace, charm, and skill superior to those of other nonhuman mammals. Ancient writers such as Pliny wrote at great length about the elephant's sense of religion, doing much to propagate the rumour that elephants worship the moon, the sun, the stars, and various other astral bodies. It appears now that none of these writers was ever present at such religious ceremonies. Those who are amazed at the elephant's intelligence, cunning and longevity have never attempted to train one, have never observed the ease with which they can be deceived, and have not examined available life-span documentation.

4. Carrington, in 1959, devised an intelligence test for elephants. It is absurdly simple, requiring only that the elephant learn to discriminate between two boxes, one with a square on its lid, and the other with a circle. The box with the square always contains food. True, some elephants appear to solve this problem relatively quickly. In general, however, their intelligence appears to be remarkably inferior to that of even a very young child. They require an average of 330 trials before they appear to know without doubt where the food is.

5. Their reputed cunning is a laughable matter among Indians, who have long been successful in capturing these mighty beasts in the simplest of manners. The elephants are herded quietly into a funnel-shaped arrangement of corrals, eventually becoming trapped in a single, larger corral. Escape would be extremely easy for a more cunning animal, requiring only that the beast walk through the fragile corral wall and wander off into the jungle. And it does happen that one of these beasts will sometimes stupidly ram its body against the wall, thereby escaping. But none of the other elephants follow, the problem seemingly being too complex. There is always ample time to repair the damage.

6. Elephants do not live several hundred years. Indeed, we live longer than they do. Even when elephants are adequately nourished, protected from the elements and from predators, and given the benefit of expert veterinary service, they never live into their eighties. The oldest elephant, whose age could be verified, died at the age of sixty-nine. Most die in their fifties or sixties. They would surely not live any

▶ QUESTIONS

1 Paragraph 1 mentions two types of memory.
   a What is thought to be the difference between having a memory like an elephant, and a memory like a sieve? **2/1/0**
   b What word in the first paragraph tells you that this belief about an elephant's memory is not accurate? **2/0**

2 Look again at paragraphs 2 and 3.
   a In your own words, write down *three* pieces of information about an elephant that are accurate. **2/1/0**
   b What is the meaning of the word 'longevity' in paragraph 3? Give a phrase from the same paragraph that helped you to answer. **2/1/0**
   c What do all the pieces of information in paragraph 3 have in common? **2/0**
   d What is the difference between the information in paragraph 2 and the information in paragraph 3? **2/0**

3 a Below is a list of statements about Carrington's intelligence tests (paragraph 4). Choose the one you think best describes what Carrington was trying to prove.
   A Elephants have a poor sense of smell
   B Elephants are not especially greedy animals
   C Elephants have a very slow understanding
   D Elephants will only eat food from a box with a square on it
   E Elephants prefer squares to circles
   F Elephants think in the same way as very young children. **2/0**

   b What is the effect of using the word 'even' in the second last sentence of paragraph 4? **2/0**

4 Look again at paragraph 5.
   a Why do Indians believe that elephants are not cunning? **2/1/0**
   b Do elephants learn by example? Give a reason for your answer. **2/1/0**
   c Why is it important that the author writes 'stupidly' to describe the elephant ramming the wall? **2/0**

5 Look once more at paragraph 6.
   a Give *three* possible risks to elephants in the wild. Use your own words. **2/1/0**
   b Apart from the removal of risks, what other help is given to elephants in captivity? **2/0**

6 a What point is the author making in the last sentence of the passage. **2/0**
   b How does he support this point? **2/1/0**

7 Explain in your own words the connection between the last sentence of paragraph 3 and the remainder of the passage. **2/1/0**

8 a What is the author trying to argue in this passage? **2/0**
   b Do you think he has been successful? Give a reason for your answer. **2/1/0**

9 a After reading the whole passage, in what way do you think the author is prejudiced towards elephants — for or against them? **2/0**
   b Give a piece of evidence used by the author to support your answer. **2/0**

GENERAL LEVEL TEST 5
The Lost Boy
George Mackay Brown

This passage is a complete short story titled *The Lost Boy*, written by George Mackay Brown. The test appears as it would in the Standard Grade exam. Try to complete it in no more than fifty minutes. There are no study notes for this test. You can use it to check how well you are progressing in your reading development.

Spaces have been left for the answers to show you how the exam paper will look. In the exam you will write your answers in the spaces provided. *If this book belongs to your school please do not write in it.*

This 'paper' would assess Grades 3 and 4 for a Standard Grade General Level award.

Read the following passage carefully. It is a short story which tells about a particular Christmas Eve for a young boy living on one of the islands of Orkney.

When you have read it — and it will help if you read it through twice — you should go on to answer the questions.

Try to answer all the questions.

1   There was one light in the village on Christmas Eve: it came from Jock Scabra's cottage, and he was the awkwardest old man that had ever lived in our village or in the island, or in the whole of Orkney.

2   I was feeling very wretched and very ill-natured myself that evening. My Aunty Belle had just been explaining to me after tea that Santa Claus, if he did exist, was a spirit that moved people's hearts to generosity and goodwill; no more or less.

3   Gone was my fat, apple-cheeked, red-coated friend of the past ten winters. Scattered were the reindeer, broken the sledge that had beaten such a marvellous path through the constellations and the Merry Dancers, while all the children of Orkney slept. Those merry perilous descents down the lum, Yule eve by Yule eve, with the sack of toys and books, games and chocolate boxes, had never really taken place at all... I looked over towards our hearth, after my aunt had finished speaking: the magic had left it, it was only a place of peat flames and peat smoke.

4   I can't tell you how angry I was, the more I thought about it. How deceitful, how cruel grown-ups were! They had exiled my dear old friend, Santa Claus, to eternal oblivion. The gifts I would find in my stocking next morning would have issued from Aunty Belle's 'spirit of generosity'. It was not the same thing at all. (Most of the year I saw little enough of that spirit of generosity — at Hallowe'en, for example, she had boxed my ears till I saw stars that had never been in the sky, for stealing a few apples and nuts out of the cupboard, before 'dooking' time.)

5   If there was a more ill-tempered person than my Aunty Belle in the village, it was, as I said, old Jock Scabra, the fisherman with a silver ring in his ear and a fierce, one-eyed tom cat.

6   His house, alone in the village, was lit that night. I saw it from our

7   Aunty Belle's piece of common sense had so angered me, that I was in a state of rebellion and recklessness. No, I would *not* sleep. I would not even stay in a house from which Santa had been banished. I felt utterly betrayed and bereaved.

8   When, about half past ten, I heard rending snores coming from Aunty Belle's bedroom, I got out of bed stealthily and put my cold clothes on and unlatched the front door and went outside. The whole house had betrayed me — well, I intended to be out of the treacherous house when the magic hour of midnight struck.

9   The road through the village was deep in snow, dark except where under old Scabra's window the lamplight had stained it an orange colour. The snow shadows were blue under his walls. The stars were like sharp nails. Even though I had wrapped my scarf round my neck, I shivered in the bitter night.

10 Where could I go? The light in the old villain's window was entrancing — I fluttered towards it like a moth. How would such a sour old creature be celebrating Christmas Eve? Thinking black thoughts, beside his embers, stroking his wicked, one-eyed cat.

11 The snow crashed like thin fragile glass under my feet.

12 I stood at last outside the fisherman's window. I looked in.

13 What I saw was astonishing beyond ghosts or trows.

14 There was no crotchety old man inside, no one-eyed cat, no ingrained filth and hung cobwebs. The paraffin lamp threw a circle of soft light, and all that was gathered inside that radiance was clean and pristine: the cups and plates on the dresser, the clock and ship-in-the-bottle and tea-caddies on the mantelpiece, the framed picture of Queen Victoria on the wall, the blue stones of the floor, the wood and straw of the fireside chair, the patchwork quilt on the bed.

15 A boy I had never seen before was sitting at the table. He might have been about my own age, and his head was a mass of bronze ringlets. On the table in front of him were an apple, an orange, a little sailing ship crudely cut from wood, with linen sails, probably cut from an old shirt. The boy — whoever he was — considered those objects with the utmost gravity. Once he put out his finger and touched the hull of the toy ship; if it was so precious it had to be treated with special delicacy, lest it broke like a soap-bubble. I couldn't see the boy's face — only his bright hair, his lissom neck and the gravity and joy that informed all his gestures. These were his meagre Christmas presents; silently he rejoiced in them.

16 Beyond the circle of lamp-light, were there other dwellers in the house? There may have been hidden breath in the darkened box bed in the corner.

17 I don't know how long I stood in the bitter night outside. My hands were trembling. I looked down at them — they were blue with cold.

18 Then suddenly, for a second, the boy inside the house turned his face to the window. Perhaps he had heard the tiny splinterings of snow under my boots, or my quickened heart-beats.

19 The face that looked at me was Jock Scabra's, but Jock Scabra's from far back at the pure source of his life, sixty winters ago, before the ring was in his ear and before bad temper and perversity had grained black lines and furrows into his face. It was as if a cloth had been taken to a tarnished web-clogged mirror.

20 The boy turned back smiling to his Christmas hoard.

21 I turned and went home. I lifted the latch quietly, not to waken Aunty Belle — for, if she knew what I had been up to that midnight, there would have been little of her 'spirit of generosity' for me. I crept, trembling, into bed.

22 When I woke up on Christmas morning, the 'spirit of the season' had loaded my stocking and the chair beside the bed with boxes of sweets,

a *Guinness Book of Records*, a digital watch, a game of space wars, a cowboy hat, and a fifty pence piece. Aunty Belle stood at my bedroom door, smiling. And 'A merry Christmas,' she said.

23   Breakfast over, I couldn't wait to get back to the Scabra house. The village was taken over by children with apples, snowballs, laughter as bright as bells.

24   I peered in at the window. All was as it had been. The piratical old man sluiced the last of his breakfast tea down his throat from a cracked saucer. He fell to picking his black-and-yellow teeth with a kipper-bone. His house was like a midden.

25   The one-eyed cat yawned wickedly beside the new flames in the hearth.

QUESTIONS

1 a At the time the story takes place, where did the story-teller live?

   b Who looked after him?

   c How old was he when the story took place? Give evidence from the passage to support your answer.

   d In your own words, say how the story-teller is feeling at the start of the story.

2 a In paragraph 2 Aunty Belle decides to explain about Santa Claus to the story-teller and her words affect him in several ways mentioned in paragraph 3. Explain what three of these effects are in your own words.

      (i) _____

      (ii) _____

      (iii) _____

   b How does Aunty Belle's explanation affect the story-teller's view of grown-ups in general?

c Why does he think of grown-ups in this way?

_____

_____

d What is the story-teller's opinion of Aunty Belle in particular? Give *two* examples from the passage that help him to form this opinion.

_____

_____

_____

_____

e What is Aunty Belle's view of what she has done? Quote from the passage to support your answer.

_____

_____

_____

3 The story-teller says he felt 'utterly betrayed and bereaved' (paragraph 7). Why should he use the word 'bereaved' to describe his feelings?

_____

_____

4 A number of events happen during this Christmas Eve. In the table below, fill in the approximate time each of the events listed took place. Beside that, quote the piece of the passage that helped you to state the correct time of each event.

Event	Time	Evidence
(i) Aunty Belle explains about Santa Claus to the story-teller		
(ii) The story-teller sneaks out of bed		
(iii) He notices a light in Jock Scabra's window		
(iv) The boy in Jock's house sees the story-teller at the window.		

5 a What did the story-teller take as a sign that he could sneak out of bed?

_____

44

b Had he been waiting long for this sign? Give a reason for your answer.

_____

_____

6 The story-teller is fond of using very descriptive statements. Below are two examples that he uses. In your own words say why each statement is appropriate.
  a 'The stars were like sharp nails.' (paragraph 9)

_____

_____

  b 'The light in the old villain's window was entrancing — I fluttered towards it like a moth.' (paragraph 10)

_____

_____

7 There is a contrast between what the story-teller expects to see in Jock Scabra's house, and what he actually does see. To show this contrast, complete the table below.

What he expects to see	What he does see
(i) 'a sour, old creature' (paragraph 10)	
(ii)	'all ... clean and pristine' (paragraph 14)

8 a How many Christmas presents had the boy in Jock Scabra's house been given?

_____

  b These presents are described as 'meagre' (paragraph 15). Do you think this is how the boy would see them? Give a reason for your answer.

_____

_____

9 Why does the story-teller say that the face of the boy came from 'a *pure* source' (paragraph 19)?

_____

_____

10 Give *two* reasons why the story-teller returns to his bed 'trembling' (paragraph 21).

(i) _____

(ii) _____

11 a In paragraph 23, the story-teller says he couldn't wait to get back to the Scabra house. Suggest *one* reason why this was so.

_____

_____

b In your opinion, do you think he is disappointed by what he sees in the morning? Give a reason for your answer.

_____

_____

12 Give *two* possible meanings for calling the story 'The Lost Boy'.

(i) _____

(ii) _____

[END OF QUESTION PAPER]

CREDIT LEVEL TEST 1
The School Experience
J. K. Scobbie

Using the double-read method, read the following passage before going on to answer the questions which follow. The passage is about the wearing of school uniforms, and the various arguments surrounding this issue. It is taken from the book *The School Experience* by J. K. Scobbie, which was written almost ten years ago, when the issue was under a great deal of discussion. If you are in difficulty, you can always find help in the study notes which appear in Chapter 4.

1   The outward symbol of school loyalty is the wearing of the school uniform. Modern educationists are mainly against it. Abolition is one of the planks in the political policy of 'pupil-power'. The arguments of the abolitionists seem to be, first, that the wearing of uniform is an authoritarian means of emphasising the master/slave relationship of staff and pupils; second, that it limits the field of personal preference, of expressing individuality, of the right to choose; third, that it emphasises social or economic or class distinctions (since, they argue, the poorer child cannot afford a uniform), and this, in turn, widens the gap between the two nations in the school and helps to create rebels.

2   The last of these arguments is certainly not valid. In most secondary schools practically all the first year intake are dressed in school uniform; it is about the end of second year that many pupils abandon it. (Incidentally, the clothes chosen to replace the uniform are usually every bit as expensive.) The change in dress betokens a change of attitude to the school. The desire to change over to something 'trendy', or to garments typifying adherence to some teenage pop cult, has become stronger than loyalty to the school. Or to put it another way—the school has not proved itself good enough to deserve the pupil's loyalty. The change represents a challenge to the school. If the school can present itself to the pupils as an honourable commonwealth, where all are of equal status and the needs of all are cared for, if it is happy, vigorous and prolific of opportunities for rich, full living at a multitude of levels, academic, recreational, aesthetic and social, then the pupils will not discard the uniform which they wore proudly on the day of enrolment as citizens of 'no mean city'.

3   The argument that pupils wish to express their individuality by choosing their own school dress is unconvincing. If they must so express themselves, they have every evening and weekend to do so. To change dress at such times may heighten the pleasure by contrast. This so-called urge to express their individuality in dress is not at all apparent when hundreds of them adopt the colours of the local team on Saturday afternoons, or when they willingly accept the uniform of Boy's Brigade or Scouts or Guides or Army Cadets or the local brass band or the dress of the pop group in which they play or indeed when they change *en masse* into jeans, the uniform of dissident youth. So far from expressing their personalities by dress they mostly seem ready to accept all sorts of uniforms or badges to identify themselves with clubs, societies, cults, etc. The question is not whether self-expression should be encouraged, it is rather whether their school is important to them.

4   The economic argument need not detain us. Many schools have a

5   The argument that school uniform is a means of maintaining slavish obedience to the staff has no basis in reality. Thousands of sports organisations in the land have their own individual blazers and ties, social clubs have their badges; our international teams, for any kind of contest, sally forth immaculately uniformed and one could extend the list of examples indefinitely. In no one of these cases could it be argued that the object was authoritarian. One wears a uniform to express not subservience but pride in being a member of an honourable institution. So it is with school uniform, or should be. But perhaps pride is one of the emotions that the sociologists wish to outlaw from schools. It is suspect; it is the language of the heart, not the clinic.

6   There are many advantages in the wearing of school uniform. As the pupils move from school into the shopping centre of the town, their presence is recognised by members of the public, and the school becomes a visible component of the larger community, a positive element not to be ignored. The pupils know that the tone of their school is in high repute; there may be an element of pride in being identified with it.

7   Within the school the wearing of uniforms nullifies any inclination a pupil might have had to 'show off' by wearing expensive clothing or by sporting the bizarre outfits of the pop cult currently in vogue.

8   Those who support the right of pupils to come to school in casual dress are really arguing for casualness in work and in behaviour. Appropriately dressed people, neat and trim, look as if they mean business and suggest efficiency and professionalism. Is there anything wrong with school pupils looking (and, one hopes, feeling) the same? Our society can hardly be thought to have benefited from twenty years of casualness.

9   A good school punctuates the session by a number of traditional occasions, some of which involve an element of ceremony, some internal, others public. There may be religious services, inauguration of office-bearers, closing ceremonies. The impact of these memorable occasions may be aesthetically enhanced by the colour of a thousand uniforms. That same beauty transforms the drabbest school corridor as the columns move from room to room. Thus will the school be remembered far in the future.

10   The main argument in favour of uniform is that its use confirms the feeling of school fellowship, the occupancy of common ground, the sense of the warmth of friendship, company on the journey. Many of our fellow human beings would give a lot for that.

▶ QUESTIONS

1 a Paragraph 1 serves *two* purposes in the passage. Name these purposes. **2/1/0**

  b Explain in your own words the relationship between paragraph 1 and the next four paragraphs. **2/0**

  c Explain in your own words the difference between paragraphs 1–5 and paragraphs 6–10. **2/0**

2 a What is meant by the sentence 'Abolition is one of the planks in the political policy of "pupil-power",' (paragraph 1)? **2/1/0**

  b From what is said in paragraph 1, who might be likely to be 'abolitionists'? **2/0**

3 a The writer picks out *three* main arguments against wearing school uniform. Explain each argument in your own words. **2/0, 2/0, 2/0**

  b From your reading of the third argument, can you suggest who might belong to the 'two nations in the school' mentioned by the writer? **2/0**

4 Look again at paragraph 2.
   a What feature of the first year intake in the writer's view makes the third argument of abolitionists invalid? **2/0**
   b Why should this feature prove the abolitionists' argument wrong? **2/1/0**
   c What *two* actions by the school does the writer suggest should be taken to prevent pupils abandoning school uniforms? Use your own words. **2/1/0**

5 a Name *three* separate things which young people do that proves the argument about expressing individuality is not completely convincing. **2/1/0**
   b In your own words, explain how all of these activities make the argument unconvincing. **2/1/0**

6 a What is meant by the word 'stigma' in paragraph 4? **2/0**
   b What word earlier in the paragraph suggests that no stigma is involved? **2/0**

7 a Based on your reading of paragraph 5, suggest a reason for the writer's choice of the phrase 'sally forth'. **2/0**
   b What two words in paragraph 5 continue the idea contained in the phrase 'slavish obedience', used in its opening sentence? **2/1/0**
   c What is the writer's opinion of sociologists? Support your answer using evidence from the text. **2/1/0**

8 The writer lists five functions performed by the wearing of school uniforms. Choose *three* of these, state in which paragraph each is to be found, and explain each of your chosen three in your own words. **2/0, 2/0, 2/0**

9 The writer is fond of using inverted commas. Find *two* examples of this and explain in each case why he uses them. **2/1/0**

10 Are you convinced by the writer's argument? Give a reason for your answer. **2/1/0**

CREDIT LEVEL TEST 2
The Sweat Lodge
Guy Lefrançois

Using the double-read method, read the following passage and then answer the questions which follow. It is about taking part in a North American Indian ceremony and is from a book called *Psychology* by Guy Lefrançois. If you are finding the test difficult, look at the study notes in Chapter 4.

1   On a bitterly cold night last January, I spoke to my grandfathers. More than that, I implored them to help me: I wailed and screeched, spluttered and babbled, moaned and whispered. Perhaps I even chanted a little: 'Ayai-yai-yai-yai.'

2   I had come to a Cree Indian sweat lodge—my first such experience and, thus far, my last. The sweat lodge is among the most fascinating of the spiritual and cultural rituals of the North American Plains Indians; when asked whether I would like to participate in a 'sweat' I scarcely hesitated. The plain truth is that I knew too little about the experience to hesitate. More honestly, I knew virtually nothing.

3   We arrive in silence, my 'host' for the evening having decided that I should experience the sweat without any preconceived notions. Previously we had purchased tobacco and cloth. Now we sit in a loosely defined circle on the floor of the medicine man's home, wrapping the tobacco in bright squares of cloth so that we might make an offering to the grandfathers. At the appointed time we shed our clothing and file out of the house, barefoot and naked, carrying our tobacco offerings through the snow to the lodge, about thirty yards away. The sweat lodge is a circular, dome-shaped affair, perhaps ten feet in diameter and no more than four feet high at its apex. It is constructed entirely of animal hides stretched tightly over a wooden frame. There is but a single small doorway covered with four or five layers of animal skins. To enter, we must get down on our hands and knees and crawl in. But first, all participants must walk three times clockwise around the fire before the hut. By now the fire is a bed of smoldering embers. It has burned all day, heating the stones that have just recently been removed and placed in the pit in the very center of the sweat lodge.

4   Thrice around the fire and past the buffalo skulls, naked and shivering; kneeling and crawling inside; handing the offering to the medicine man, who hangs it with the others amid the poplar rafters. The heat is startling, intense. We sit cross-legged around the fire pit, backs to the wall. There are no windows, no cracks in the lodge. Light filters dimly through the partially open doorway. My legs are cramped, awkward. The heat is intense but still welcome.

5   There are ceremonies before the sweat, and for these the main door flap remains open. Inside, the medicine man lights a bunch of sweetgrass, an herb that grows wild on the plains of the northern United States and southern Canada. It smolders, filling the lodge with its pungent incense. The sweetgrass passes from hand to hand around the circle, each of us wafting it deliberately to and fro several times before passing it on, clockwise. The medicine man finally receives it again and discards it. He lights the peace pipe and draws deeply of its smoke before passing it on. It too must go around the circle; and we each taste the sweet smoke before the pipe is laid beside the sweetgrass. A wooden gourd is now dipped into a water container. The

medicine man sips sparingly and pours a few cold drops on his head and back; we all sip and sprinkle in turn, and our skins shiver slightly at the rude, cold touch.

6   'Let the sweat begin!' The medicine man's sudden shout startles me. The outside flaps are dropped into place and the lodge is pitched into sudden and almost absolute blackness—almost but not quite, for the feverishly heated rocks in the center pit glow eerily. And although we can see them, they do not provide enough light to enable us to see anything else.

7   The temperature begins to rise at once, and the medicine man speaks. Softly at first, he asks the grandfathers for guidance and prays that each of us might have a good sweat, that we might be rid of bad thoughts and bad feelings, and that our spirits be lightened and gladdened. And as he speaks, he splashes water upon the rocks, the steam instantly scalding. By now I am drenched in perspiration and I breathe the burning air with difficulty. The medicine man begins to chant: 'Ayai-yai-yai-yai-yai; ayai-yai-yai-yai'. And others, not novices, join in. I too chant, the sound and the effort distracting me from my discomfort.

8   We pray then, each person individually but aloud, imploring the grandfathers to help us. 'Help me, grandfathers ... ayai-yai-yai-yai.' The heat continues to rise, and soon people moan and groan, some swaying from side to side, others bent over, trying to suck cooler air from the earthen floor. With the rising heat, the volume of discordant voices also rises—the chants and implorations, the words *grandfather ... grandfathers*, the moaning and the scarcely disguised screams—until, when I am certain that I can stand it no longer, the medicine man shouts, 'Open the door'.

9   The cold air sifts in slowly, and we bend low to the ground so that we might breathe it. 'It is done,' I think to myself, 'I have done it.'

10   But it is not done. After only a few minutes, the medicine man asks that the door be shut, and the sweat begins again. This time it is longer and more painful, the supplications are less restrained, and I begin to panic toward the end, realizing that there is no easy and fast way out of the lodge except over the glowing hot stones. Finally the medicine man again provides short-lived relief, before we begin the third sweat. And there is a fourth as well. One of the younger Indian lads, recently recovering from some sickness, is forced to leave before the fourth sweat. The medicine man tells us that there is no shame, no dishonor, in having to leave the sweat. Sometimes when you are not right in your body or your spirit, the ordeal is too great and the grandfathers cannot help you enough that you might stay and benefit from the whole sweat. Sometimes it is better to leave. I agree silently, but remain seated on the sweat-soaked earth. Perhaps I am beginning to hallucinate. During the fourth sweat, when the medicine man speaks of the eagle feathers, I distinctly sense a swift light stroke across my left foot. Frantically I search the darkness with my hands to discover what has touched me. Somebody's hair, perhaps. But there is nothing. In agony now, I half lie on the earth, my head turned away from the rock pit, my mouth at the far lower reaches of the lodge, trying desperately to fill my lungs with fresh air. There is none. I hold my breath but find that I have done that too many times already. My body screams for oxygen, my skin hurts from the heat, and every pore is clogged with perspiration, but the heavy air will evaporate no more. When I scream to the grandfathers, the scream is not a ritual—an empty sound sanctified by tradition. It is real; I scream for help.

11   'Open the doors'. It is done and we file once more around the fire and

12   Later I speak with the medicine man, trying to discover why people willingly suffer the sweats. It does different things for different people, I am told, and these things cannot always be put into words. There is much in life that can only be sensed; much that is as conscious and as real as anything that you or I might touch or say, but that can neither be touched nor put into words. There is much that is beyond our ordinary and our scientific comprehension; and perhaps there are things that are neither conscious nor unconscious. Words, logic, and science might not always be enough.

►QUESTIONS

1 The first paragraph consists of three sentences. As you move from first to third, the content becomes more and more unusual.
   a Explain what is unusual about the first sentence. **2/0**
   b What does 'implored' mean in the second sentence? **2/0**
   c What do you notice about the words in sentence two that describe how the writer implored? **2/1/0**
   d What do these phrases tell you about the writer's emotional state at the time? **2/0**
   e What word in the third sentence tells you that chanting was, in the writer's opinion, the most unusual of all the activities mentioned in paragraph 1? **2/0**

2 Paragraph 2 tells you why the writer behaved so strangely in paragraph 1.
   a How does it affect the overall opening of the passage to describe the behaviour before explaining it? **2/1/0**
   b The writer says in paragraph 2 that he 'scarcely hesitated' to agree to taking part in the sweat. What *two* reasons does he give for agreeing so quickly? **2/1/0**
   c Is there any possibility that the writer would do the same thing again? Give a phrase in paragraph 2 which helped you to decide. **2/1/0**

3 a In paragraph 3 the writer begins to use the present tense. Suggest a reason for this. **2/1/0**
   b In your own words, explain why the participants in the sweat arrive in silence. **2/0**
   c Before moving to the sweat lodge, the participants do *three* things in preparation for the sweat. List these. **2/1/0**

4 Read paragraphs 3 and 4 again. From the information provided in the passage, describe the following features of the sweat lodge:
   (i) Shape of floor **2/0**
   (ii) Height of lodge **2/0**
   (iii) Breadth **2/0**
   (iv) Decoration, if any **2/0**
   (v) Material of frame (state type) **2/1/0**
   (vi) Material of covering **2/0**
   (vii) Number of windows **2/0**
   (viii) Number of doors **2/0**
   (ix) Contents of lodge, if any (state location) **2/1/0**

5 When the writer enters the sweat lodge (paragraph 4), at first he is both comfortable and uncomfortable.
   a In what way does he feel comfortable and why should this be? **2/1/0**
   b In what way is he uncomfortable and why is this? **2/1/0**

6 Describe the *three* main ceremonies mentioned in paragraph 5, performed *before* the sweat actually begins? **2/1/0**

7 Read paragraph 6 once more.
   a Once the sweat begins what prevents the lodge from being completely dark inside? **2/0**
   b Why is 'feverishly' an effective word to explain what had happened to the rocks? **2/1/0**
   c How do you think the author feels just after the flaps have been dropped? Give a word in paragraph 6 which helps you to decide. **2/1/0**

8 You are told in paragraph 7 that there is a change in temperature. *Two* other changes also take place in this paragraph.
   a State in your own words what these two changes are. **2/1/0**

b Give evidence from paragraph 7 that these changes have taken place.
2/1/0

c At the end of paragraph 7 why does the writer make the point that it is 'not novices' who join in the chanting?
2/1/0

9 Look again at paragraph 8. It begins 'We pray then, ...' The word 'then' can be called a structuring word because it tells you that what follows is a new stage of the ritual, that of praying to the grandfathers.

a *Two other* stages of the ritual are introduced in this paragraph. In your own words explain what happens at each of these stages.
2/0, 2/0

b Write down the structuring words used to indicate when each stage was to follow.
2/0, 2/0

10 By thinking about its content and its relationship to paragraphs 8 and 10, state why paragraph 9 should be so short.
2/1/0

11 a Explain in your own words what the writer and the medicine man agree about in paragraph 10.
2/1/0

b Why do you think the writer chooses to agree 'silently'?
2/1/0

12 Midway through paragraph 10, the tone of the writer changes from being certain, to being uncertain about what is taking place.

a What sentence marks the beginning of this change?
2/0

b Not only does the tone change, the writer's attitude to the sweat has changed. What word, used in both paragraph 2 and paragraph 10, helps to convey this change of attitude?
2/0

c Explain in your own words what the change in attitude is.
2/1/0

13 Paragraph 12 offers two views of the sweat. One is the view of the Cree Indian medicine man. The other is the writer's.

a In your own words, say what each one believes about the sweat.
2/1/0, 2/1/0

b What type of job might the writer have? Quote from paragraph 12 to support your answer.
2/1/0

14 Having read the whole passage, give one reason why the writer chooses to put the word 'host' (paragraph 3) in inverted commas.
2/1/0

CREDIT LEVEL TEST 3
Porphyria's Lover
Robert Browning

Using the double-read method, read the following poem and then answer the questions which follow. It is about a rather unusual murder committed by the speaker of the poem. The poem is called *Porphyria's Lover* and was written by Robert Browning.

The questions are divided into *three* sections:

▶ **SECTION 1** asks only about lines 1–30 of the poem.

▶ **SECTION 2** asks only about lines 31–60 of the poem.

▶ **SECTION 3** asks about the whole poem.

If you are having difficulty, look at the study notes in Chapter 4.

        The rain set early in tonight,
           The sullen wind was soon awake,
        It tore the elm-tops down for spite,
           And did its worst to vex the lake:
5   I listened with heart fit to break,
        When glided in Porphyria; straight
           She shut the cold out and the storm,
        And kneeled and made the cheerless grate
           Blaze up, and all the cottage warm;
10   Which done, she rose, and from her form
        Withdrew the dripping cloak and shawl,
           And laid her soiled gloves by, untied
        Her hat and let the damp hair fall,
           And, last, she sat down by my side
15   And called me. When no voice replied,
        She put my arm about her waist,
           And made her smooth white shoulder bare,
        And all her yellow hair displaced,
           And, stooping, made my cheek lie there,
20   And spread o'er all her yellow hair,
        Murmuring how she loved me — she
           Too weak, for all her heart's endeavour,
        To set its struggling passion free
           From pride, and vainer ties dissever,
25   And give herself to me forever.
        But passion sometimes would prevail,
           Nor could tonight's gay feast restrain
        A sudden thought of one so pale
           For love of her, and all in vain:
30   So, she was come through wind and rain.
        Be sure I looked up at her eyes
           Happy and proud; at last I knew
        Porphyria worshipped me; surprise
           Made my heart swell, and still it grew
35   While I debated what to do.
        That moment she was mine, mine, fair,
           Perfectly pure and good: I found
        A thing to do, and all her hair
           In one long yellow string I wound

40 Three times her little throat around,
    And strangled her. No pain felt she;
    I am quite sure she felt no pain.
    As a shut bud that holds a bee,
    I warily oped her lids: again
45 Laughed the blue eyes without a stain.
    And I untightened next the tress
    About her neck; her cheek once more
    Blushed bright beneath my burning kiss:
    I propped her head up as before,
50 Only, this time my shoulder bore
    Her head, which droops upon it still:
    The smiling rosy little head,
    So glad it has its utmost will,
    That all it scorned at once is fled,
55 And I, its love, am gained instead!
    Porphyria's love: she guessed not how
    Her darling one wish would be heard.
    And thus we sit together now,
    And all night long we have not stirred,
60 And yet God has not said a word!

▶SECTION ONE QUESTIONS

All the questions in this section deal with lines 1–30.

1 a In what way is the wind described in lines 2–4? **2/1/0**
   b Give *two* separate words from lines 2–4 that help you to answer question **1a**. **2/1/0**

2 a In what way does Porphyria, in lines 5–9, contrast with the speaker of the poem? **2/0**
   b Give *two* reasons why the poet chooses to describe the fireplace as 'the cheerless grate' (line 8). **2/1/0**

3 a What is especially noticeable about the behaviour of the speaker in the first nineteen lines of the poem? **2/0**
   b What might this suggest about his attitude at that time towards Porphyria? **2/0**
   c Give *two* pieces of evidence from lines 1–19 to support your answer to question **3b**. **2/1/0**

4 a What conflict does the speaker believe exists in Porphyria? **2/0**
   b Is there any evidence of this conflict in Porphyria's behaviour? Support your

   c Which side of the conflict does the speaker believe prevents Porphyria giving herself to him forever? **2/0**

5 a Did the speaker expect to see Porphyria on this particular night? **2/0**
   b By close reference to the poem, give *two* reasons for your answer to question **5a**. **2/1/0**

6 Porphyria has said that she loves the speaker, so why should he still believe that his love for her is 'all in vain' (line 29)? Support your answer with evidence from the poem. **2/1/0**

▶SECTION TWO QUESTIONS

All the questions in this section deal with lines 31–60.

1 Explain in your own words why the speaker wants you to 'Be sure' (line 31) that he felt 'Happy and proud' (line 32). **2/0**

2 From line 31 a change has come over the speaker.
   a What reason is given for this change? **2/0**
   b The change begins with the speaker feeling a mixture of emotions; happi-

mentioned. Name two other emotions he feels here. **2/1/0**

c In what general way does the speaker change? **2/0**

3 a What does the poet hope to show by having the speaker use repetition in line 36? **2/0**

b Explain in your own words how this repetition might act as a warning of what will follow immediately. **2/0**

4 a What is the effect of having the speaker describe Porphyria's murder in very simple language? **2/1/0**

b After he has committed the murder, the speaker does *four* things. List these. **2/1/0**

c What influence do these four actions have on the way you feel towards the speaker? **2/0**

5 a As you are reading you should gradually form an impression of the setting. What changes in line 51? **2/0**

b Explain in your own words how the change in line 51 affects the place you imagine yourself to be as you read the poem. **2/0**

▶ **SECTION THREE   QUESTIONS**

The questions in this section cover the whole poem.

1 In what way does the description of the weather in lines 1–4 prepare you for what happens later in the poem? **2/0**

2 The poem suggests, but does not state, the reason why the speaker murders Porphyria. Several key phrases allow you to guess at a possible motive for the crime. Below are three such phrases. Explain in your own words a possible motive suggested by the combination of these phrases.
'Too weak' (line 22)
'vainer ties' (line 24)
'That moment she was mine' (line 36) **2/1/0**

3 a What alternative is offered by the speaker to 'all it scorned' (line 54)? **2/0**

b What word tells you that this is an alternative? **2/0**

c What does the speaker believe is scorned by Porphyria? **2/0**

d How had this been referred to earlier in the poem? **2/0**

e Each of these references suggests a different attitude. Explain this difference. **2/1/0**

4 Do you think the speaker is sure that he was right to murder Porphyria? Give a reason for your answer. **2/1/0**

CREDIT LEVEL TEST 4
Great Expectations
Charles Dickens

Using the double-read method, go through the passage below before answering the questions which follow.

This passage is taken from the novel *Great Expectations* by Charles Dickens. It describes a terrifying meeting between the hero of the book, Pip, and a 'fearful man' called Magwitch.

If you are finding the passage difficult, take a look at the study notes in Chapter 4.

1   'Hold your noise!' cried a terrible voice, as a man started up from among the graves at the side of the church porch. 'Keep still, you little devil, or I'll cut your throat!'

2   A fearful man, all in coarse gray, with a great iron on his leg. A man with no hat, and with broken shoes, and with an old rag tied round his head. A man who had been soaked in water, and smothered in mud, and lamed by stones, and cut by flints, and stung by nettles, and torn by briars; who limped, and shivered, and glared and growled; and whose teeth chattered in his head as he seized me by the chin.

3   'Oh! Don't cut my throat, sir,' I pleaded in terror. 'Pray don't do it, sir.'

4   'Tell us your name!' said the man. 'Quick!'

5   'Pip, sir.'

6   'Once more,' said the man, staring at me. 'Give it mouth!'

7   'Pip. Pip, sir.'

8   'Show us where you live,' said the man. 'Pint out the place!'

9   I pointed to where our village lay, on the flat inshore among the alder-trees and pollards, a mile or more from the church.

10 The man, after looking at me for a moment, turned me upside-down, and emptied my pockets. There was nothing in them but a piece of bread. When the church came to itself—for he was so sudden and strong that he made it go head over heels before me, and I saw the steeple under my feet—when the church came to itself, I say, I was seated on a high tombstone, trembling, while he ate the bread ravenously.

11 'You young dog,' said the man, licking his lips, 'what fat cheeks you ha' got.'

12 I believe they were fat, though I was at that time undersized for my years, and not strong.

13 'Darn me if I couldn't eat 'em,' said the man, with a threatening shake of his head, 'and if I han't half a mind to't!'

14 I earnestly expressed my hope that he wouldn't, and held tighter to the tombstone on which he had put me; partly to keep myself upon it; partly, to keep myself from crying.

15 'Now then, lookee here!' said the man. 'Where's your mother?'

16 'There, sir!' said I.

17 He started, made a short run, and stopped and looked over his shoulder.

18 'There sir!' I timidly exclaimed, '"Also Georgiana". That's my mother.'

19 'Oh!' said he, coming back. 'And is that your father alonger your

21   'Ha!' he muttered then, considering. 'Who d'ye live with—supposin' you're kindly let to live, which I han't made up my mind about?'

22   'My sister, sir—Mrs Joe Gargery—wife of Joe Gargery, the blacksmith, sir.'

23   'Blacksmith, eh?' said he. And he looked down at his leg.

24   After darkly looking at his leg and at me several times, he came closer to my tombstone, took me by both arms, tilted me back as far as he could hold me; so that his eyes looked most powerfully down into mine, and mine looked most helplessly up into his.

25   'Now lookee here,' he said, 'the question being whether you're to be let to live. You know what a file is?'

26   'Yes, sir.'

27   'And you know what wittles is?'

28   'Yes, sir.'

29   After each question he tilted me over a little more, so as to give me a greater sense of helplessness and danger.

30   'You get me a file.' He tilted me again. 'And you get me wittles.' He tilted me again. 'You bring 'em both to me.' He tilted me again.

31   I was dreadfully frightened, and so giddy that I clung to him with both hands, and said, 'If you would kindly please to let me keep upright, sir, perhaps I shouldn't be sick, and perhaps I could attend more.'

32   He gave me a most tremendous dip and roll, so that the church jumped over its own weather-cock. Then, he held me by the arms, in an upright position on the top of the stone, and went on in these fearful terms—

33   'You bring me, to-morrow morning early, that file and them wittles. You bring the lot to me, at that old Battery over yonder. You do it, and you never dare to say a word or dare to make a sign concerning your having seen such a person as me, or any person sumever, and you shall be let to live. You fail, or you go from my words in any partickler, no matter how small it is, and your heart and your liver shall be tore out, roasted and ate. Now, I ain't alone, as you may think I am. There's a young man hid with me, in comparison with which young man I am a Angel. That young man hears the words I speak. That young man has a secret way pecooliar to himself, of getting at a boy, and at his heart, and at his liver. It is in wain for a boy to attempt to hide himself from that young man. A boy may lock his door, may be warm in bed, may tuck himself up, may draw the clothes over his head, may think himself comfortable and safe, but that young man will softly creep and creep his way to him and tear him open. I am a-keeping that young man from harming of you at the present moment, with great difficulty. I find it wery hard to hold that young man off your inside. Now, what do you say?'

34   I said that I would get him the file, and I would get him what broken bits of food I could, and I would come to him at the Battery, early in the morning.

▶ QUESTIONS

1 Look again at paragraphs 1–7.
   a Write down *three* things about the 'fearful man' that caused Pip to feel terrified. (Use your own words wherever possible.)   **2/1/0**

   b The author also tries to stir another emotion in the reader's reaction to this man. State what emotion this is and explain your answer in terms of your reading of the first seven paragraphs.   **2/1/0**

    c Give *two* examples of the man's use of incorrect English in these paragraphs. **2/1/0**

    d Why is it effective for the author to make the man talk this way? **2/0**

2 a What age do you think Pip is? **2/0**

    b What *three* pieces of evidence from paragraphs 1–12 helped you to answer question **2a**. **2/1/0**

3 Look again at paragraphs 15–21.

    a What, first of all, did the man believe with regard to Pip's mother? **2/0**

    b What behaviour tells you this? **2/1/0**

    c Suggest a reason for the man behaving this way. **2/1/0**

    d What earlier piece of information fits in with this behaviour? **2/0**

    e Why does Pip say 'Also Georgiana' (paragraph 18)? Support your answer using evidence from the passage. **2/1/0**

4 Look again at paragraphs 22–24.

    a What is the relationship between Pip and Joe? **2/0**

    b In what way is Joe's occupation likely to be useful to the man? **2/1/0**

5 a What does the word 'wittles' (paragraph 27) mean? **2/0**

    b Explain how the passage helped you to understand this word. **2/0**

6 In the passage, Pip is turned up and down by the man until he feels sick.

    a Look at Pip's speech in paragraph 31. How effective is this speech? Give a reason for your answer. **2/1/0**

    b Keeping Pip's situation in mind, why should the author choose to make Pip reply in this way, using this language? **2/1/0**

7 In paragraph 33, the author makes a lot of use of the technique called repetition. He uses it in different places for different reasons.

    a Find *two* separate examples of the author's use of repetition. **2/0**

    b For each example you have chosen, explain what the author's purpose in using repetition was. **2/1/0**

8 a Why does the man tell Pip about 'the young man' in paragraph 33? **2/1/0**

    b Does this young man exist? Give a reason for your answer. **2/1/0**

9 Write down a suitable title for this passage. **2/0**

CREDIT LEVEL TEST 5
The Mouse
Saki

This passage is taken from a short story called *The Mouse*, written by Saki.

The test appears as it would in the Standard Grade exam. Try to complete it in no more than fifty minutes. There are no study notes for this test. You can use it to check how well you are progressing in your reading development.

Spaces have been left for the answers to show you how the exam paper will look. In the exam you will write your answers in the spaces provided. *If this book belongs to your school please do not write in it.*

This 'paper' would assess Grades 1 and 2 for a Standard Grade Credit Level award.

Read the following passage carefully. It is from a short story which tells about a journey made by a man called Theoderic Voler and the part played by a mouse.

When you have read it — and it will help if you read it through twice — you should go on to answer the questions.

Try to answer all the questions.

1   Theoderic Voler had been brought up, from infancy to the confines of middle age, by a fond mother whose chief solicitude had been to keep him screened from what she called the coarser realities of life. When she died she left Theoderic alone in a world that was as real as ever, and a good deal coarser than he considered it had any need to be. To a man of his temperament and upbringing even a simple railway journey was crammed with petty annoyances and minor discords, and as he settled himself down in a second-class compartment one September morning he was conscious of ruffled feelings and general mental discomposure.

2   He had been staying at a country vicarage, the inmates of which had been certainly neither brutal nor bacchanalian, but their supervision of the domestic establishment had been of that lax order which invites disaster. The pony carriage that was to take him to the station had never been properly ordered, and when the moment for his departure drew near the handyman who should have produced the required article was nowhere to be found. In this emergency Theoderic, to his mute but very intense disgust, found himself obliged to collaborate with the vicar's daughter in the task of harnessing the pony, which necessitated groping about in an ill-lighted outhouse called a stable, and smelling very like one — except in patches where it smelt of mice. Without being actually afraid of mice, Theoderic classed them among the coarser incidents of life, and considered that Providence, with a little exercise of moral courage, might long ago have recognised that they were not indispensable, and have withdrawn them from circulation.

3   As the train glided out of the station Theoderic's nervous imagination accused himself of exhaling a weak odour of stableyard, and possibly of displaying a mouldy straw or two on his usually well-brushed garments. Fortunately the only other occupant of the compartment, a lady of about the same age as himself, seemed inclined for slumber rather than scrutiny; the train was not due to stop until the terminus was reached, in about an hour's time, and the carriage

4   was of the old-fashioned sort, that held no communication with a corridor, therefore no further travelling companions were likely to intrude on Theoderic's semi-privacy.

And yet the train had scarcely attained its normal speed before he became reluctantly but vividly aware that he was not alone with the slumbering lady; he was not even alone in his own clothes. A warm, creeping movement over his flesh betrayed the unwelcome and highly resented presence, unseen but poignant, of a strayed mouse, that had evidently dashed into its present retreat during the episode of the pony harnessing. Furtive stamps and shakes and wildly directed pinches failed to dislodge the intruder; and the lawful occupant of the clothes lay back against the cushions and endeavoured rapidly to evolve some means for putting an end to the dual ownership. It was unthinkable that he should continue for the space of a whole hour in the horrible position of a shelter for vagrant mice (already his imagination had at least doubled the numbers of the alien invasion). On the other hand, nothing less drastic than partial disrobing would ease him of his tormentor, and to undress in the presence of a lady, even for so laudable a purpose, was an idea that made his eartips tingle in a blush of abject shame.

QUESTIONS

1 a From the opening sentence, select *three* separate words which help you to understand how protective Theoderic's mother had been in bringing up her son.

(i) _____

(ii) _____

(iii) _____

b In your own words explain why she chose to bring him up in this way.

_____
_____

c Write down an adjective of your own choice to describe Theoderic's upbringing.

_____

2 In your opinion, why should the author choose to include the word 'even' (paragraph 1) in mentioning a simple railway journey?

_____
_____

3 a From evidence only found in paragraph 1, suggest the effect that 'the coarser realities of life' might have upon Theoderic.

_____

b What does this tell you about Theoderic's temperament?

_____

4 What is the link between paragraphs 1 and 2?

_____

5 Read paragraph 2 again. It is more specific than paragraph 1, and offers evidence that the 'domestic establishment' is supervised in a lax manner.

a In your own words, say what is meant by 'the domestic establishment'.

_____

_____

b There are at least four pieces of evidence that the supervision is 'of that lax order which invites disaster'. Write down *four* pieces of evidence.

(i) _____

(ii) _____

(iii) _____

(iv) _____

6 In paragraph 1, the author has mentioned 'petty annoyances' and 'minor discords', yet this contrasts with the words 'disaster' and 'emergency', in paragraph 2. In your own words, explain why there should be this change.

_____

_____

7 Why is Theoderic's disgust described as 'mute' (paragraph 2)?

_____

8 a Put the phrase 'withdrawn them from circulation' (last sentence, paragraph 2) into everyday English.

_____

b Why does the author express the idea in this fashion?

_____

9 Paragraphs 1 and 2 give you some insight into Theoderic's character. Write down, in your own words, *three* things you could tell about his character.

(i) _____

(ii) _____

(iii) _____

10 In your own words, give *two* reasons why Theoderic is not completely at ease at the start of the train journey.

_____

_____

11 There are a number of features which contribute to the predicament in which Theoderic finds himself in paragraphs 3 and 4. Two, obviously, are Theoderic's own personality and the presence of the mouse, but there are others. Name *three* others.

(i) _____

(ii) _____

(iii) _____

12 Theoderic is said to have 'a nervous imagination' (paragraph 3). Give *two* examples of this.

(i) _____

(ii) _____

13 How does the phrase 'furtive stamps and shakes' (paragraph 4), tie in with what we already know of Theoderic's character?

_____

14 a Explain in your own words the impression created by the phrase 'shelter for vagrant mice' (paragraph 4).

_____

_____

b How does this relate to the idea of being 'the lawful occupant' (paragraph 4)?

_____

15 a In your opinion, *when* is this story set?

_____

b Give *two* pieces of evidence from the passage to support your answer.

(i) _____

(ii) _____

16 What *two* possible meanings could be taken from the title of the whole passage?

(i) _____

(ii) _____

17 Briefly, in your own words, predict what the outcome of the story will be, using what you have read so far to help you.

_____

_____

_____

[END OF QUESTION PAPER]

CHAPTER · FOUR ·
STUDY NOTES ON READING TESTS

These notes should be used to help you out of difficulties. They are to help you find the answers, not to give the answers. Good luck!

STUDY NOTES ON FOUNDATION LEVEL TEST 2
The Gooseberry

This is quite a short passage, and the vocabulary is not very hard. It deals with the discovery of something unpleasant and worrying. The discovery is not made all at once. It begins with one character feeling quite uneasy, and believing something has happened, but when the second character comes along, the truth slowly emerges.

As you would expect, beliefs and fears are the main ideas in the passage, and in order to make these beliefs and fears seem real, it is important for the writer to let the reader build up a picture of the characters. You can tell a great deal about a character from the way he or she behaves and the sort of things he or she does. That is why the passage begins by creating an idea in your mind about the sort of person Herbert is.

The main areas covered by the questions, and therefore what you look for in the passage, are:

the character of Herbert; Herbert's behaviour; words to describe Herbert, his actions, his character; Rose's behaviour; information about the burglary; information about the house.

STUDY NOTES ON FOUNDATION LEVEL TEST 3
How to Complain

This passage is not a piece of fiction. It was written to offer people advice about making complaints. It deals with real situations. This means it will contain mainly *ideas, facts* and *examples*. It wants to pass on as much information as it can, and that is why it is full of instructions: 'If this happens, then you should do the following'. Look out for the frequent use of 'if... then'. These words tell you that advice on what to do is being offered.

Also, the passage is full of technical terms. This is because it is giving you a *method*, how to use the law to complain (the word 'how' tells you that the passage will mention a method or a way of doing something). The passage is dealing with the law, something which is full of exact terms only used at special times. Now, although this makes the passage difficult in places, you should remember that it also an *example* of a tricky idea. Look for explanations and examples. These can be found sometimes after phrases like 'this means that...', 'for instance', 'eg', 'for example', 'this is shown by', or 'if... then...'.

So, if you are not quite sure of an idea or a word, always look close by for an explanation or an example. Ask yourself questions like: 'What words *do* I know?' 'What is the paragraph about in general?' 'Where is the nearest explanation or example?'

Most *methods* involve *doing* things one step at a time. Look for the various things to do, and all the different steps involved. When the passage says 'Know the Law', it isn't hard to guess that you will be given facts and ideas used in the Law. Since some of the ideas could be difficult, you will also be given *explanations* and *examples* (so remember how to spot these!)

ideas; examples and explanations to make facts and ideas clearer; difficult ideas broken down into simpler, easier-to-understand, parts; giving out the information or method in carefully organised stages.

STUDY NOTES ON GENERAL LEVEL TEST 1
Scotland's Heritage

You will remember that the passage for Foundation Level Test 3, *How To Complain*, was described as a passage that dealt with information, ideas and methods. In some ways, the two pamphlets used in this test are the same. They both want the reader to gain new knowledge. Both want you to be given new ideas. However, there is one important difference. These pamphlets want *to persuade* you to join the organisations they describe.

The purpose of each pamphlet is to make the organisation sound attractive. So each writer has organised selected information and presented it to you in a way he or she hopes will make you want to join. Each offers what are called *incentives* — that is, reasons why you might want to join.

As you read the passages, try to decide what attractive offers the pamphlets are making, and *how* they hope to persuade you to join. Are they trying to be light-hearted, jokey? Are they trying to sound exciting, or interesting, or varied? What in the pamphlets do you think is there to try and attract new members into each organisation? Is it more than words? What words are the persuading words?

STUDY NOTES ON GENERAL LEVEL TEST 2
Dracula

Many people base their knowledge of the vampire, Dracula, on the Hollywood film versions of the blood-sucking Count. However, this passage is taken from the original book, and it shows that Hollywood made some changes. One of the ways this passage will test you, then, is to find out how well you can use only the words on the page, and not rely on ideas taken from the films. This should show you the importance of a golden rule of Reading tests: *do not add your own details unless asked to by the question; only use what can be found in the passage!*

What about the passage, then? You will notice that it is written in the form of a journal, which is a sort of diary. This means that it is told by one person and, like most good diaries, it contains details of the writer's *impressions* (description of places and people) and *emotions* (how the writer felt, and reasons for his feelings).

Of course, everyone knows that *Dracula* is a horror story, so one other thing you can expect from the passage is the build-up of atmosphere. How can the writer build up atmosphere? Look out for the use of several different adjectives with similar meaning: for example, count the number of times dark or darkness is used or described. Be aware of how the writing appeals to the senses of seeing, hearing, smelling, touching and tasting. This is because in real life you build up an impression of a place or a person by using these senses. The writer wants you to feel the same way as Jonathan Harker does about Dracula and his castle. He does this by having Harker describe the Count and the castle in words that relate to sight, touch, taste, smell, hearing. As you read the passage, then, ask yourself these questions. What are the sights? What does Jonathan Harker hear? How does the place smell? How would the Count's handshake affect Jonathan? Think of the tastes that he experiences. Once you have thought of this, add it all together and think of how Jonathan Harker is feeling. Think of how *you* are expected to feel, since you are seeing the Count through Jonathan's senses.

One further point. When a writer wants to create an interesting character — and Count Dracula is certainly an interesting character! — there are several ways of doing it. These ways are part of the ABC method:

Appearance
Behaviour } **C**haracter

Look at Dracula's *appearance*. It is made unique, no one else looks like that, and that always helps your interest to grow. And look at his *behaviour*: it is a mixture of very good manners and very strange and unusual ways of doing things. How much is simply politeness? And how much of it is odd and surprising?

The combination of appearance and behaviour make our character seem very alive (even Dracula!), but only if the appearance and behaviour make the character unique (like Dracula).

The main areas covered by the questions are:
the changing feelings of Jonathan Harker; the build-up of atmosphere; the words that create different moods; the impression given by Count Dracula; the strangeness of Dracula's castle.

STUDY NOTES ON GENERAL LEVEL TEST 3

Tartan Travels

This piece of personal experience writing is intended to be comical. Much of the comedy comes from the writer making fun of his own character. It is laughter at his own expense: you laugh because at the same time he is telling you he is afraid of heights, he is trying to hide the fact from his wife.

You can also see three popular techniques used in creating comic effects. These are

a the use of exaggeration,

b the deliberate creation of confusion, and

c placing two ideas side by side in an unexpected way.

Try to find examples of these techniques in the passage.

a Exaggeration is the comic art of making things out to be much bigger or better or scarier or worse than they truly are so that they become ridiculous and therefore funny. One question you might ask yourself, then, is 'Was the writer really as scared as he claims?'

b Deliberate confusion is created in several ways in this passage. First, it is created by leaving the meaning vague, open to more than one interpretation (eg look at the last two sentences of paragraph 3). Second, it is created by the use of 'red herrings', ideas that have no real bearing on the situation (eg look at the last sentence of paragraph 10).

c One of the best examples of a writer placing two ideas together in an unexpected way is in the quotation 'I'm a hero with coward's legs' (paragraph 22).

Clearly, then, one of the difficulties of this passage will be to see the humour. It is especially difficult in an exam situation because you expect exams to be a serious business and to meet a piece of comic writing can put you off-balance; you may not even recognise the

This is why you should always try to be aware of the *tone* of the passage: How seriously is the writer treating his subject? Is he exaggerating? Is she being deliberately confusing? Is the writer putting strange ideas close together?

Like most writing that deals with personal experience, this passage combines a story of events, description and explanation of feelings. The point of view is very individual, very personal and this makes the writing original.

You might find some of the vocabulary difficult. That is why the questions begin with a test of your understanding of difficult words. To help you in this, always look at the words that surround the difficult one. This is because no word operates completely on its own. Each word spreads its meaning over the words around it, each word borrows sense from its neighbours. So if you want to understand difficult words, here is an example of how to do it.

Look at the word 'impervious' in paragraph 11. It's not the easiest of words, is it? How can you find its meaning?

First, decide what kind of word it is. Is it a noun, a verb, an adjective, or something else? Well, by looking at its surroundings, you can see that it seems to describe the word 'way'. That makes it an adjective. It's a describing word.

Next, remove it from the sentence. What does that leave? What can you put in its place? '... *said* my wife in that —— way beloved of all wives when *blissfully ignoring...*' etc.

So, you can tell that it is a way of saying something; a way used by wives when they are ignoring their husbands. That means that 'impervious' describes a way of speaking that ignores what others are saying. Any ideas? A way that won't allow the words of a husband to be heard. An impervious way. You've got it.

If you can work an answer out in this way,

STUDY NOTES ON GENERAL LEVEL TEST 4
Elephants

Although it may not seem so at first glance, this passage is in fact a piece of argumentative writing. That is, the author is trying to persuade you that the view he has about elephants is correct. What do you think his view of elephants is?

One of the main features of argumentative writing is the clear and logical structure. If you can find the topic of each paragraph—the key idea—you will then notice that they come in a very definite order. This order is important because it is what makes the argument strong. In fact, in this passage the author makes a statement about elephants then goes on to examine each part of the statement in turn and in greater detail.

Another important feature of this type of writing is the careful use of evidence. In order to win you over on to his side, the author shows you interesting or unusual, but also very persuasive, pieces of information. So, as you read this passage, you should try to decide what pieces of information are facts and what are only opinions. If you can see the difference between fact and opinion in this passage, it will be much easier to understand it. Picking out the signposts to certainty (see Chapter 2) might help here!

One last point: as well as a logical structure and clever use of evidence, the author also demonstrates a very obvious attitude to elephants. In what way do you think he is prejudiced towards elephants—for or against them? To decide on this you will need to weigh up the evidence he uses and the way he orders the argument.

STUDY NOTES ON CREDIT LEVEL TEST 1
The School Experience

This is a good example of strong argumentative writing. The author is hoping to convince you that his views are correct. He begins by explaining what the controversial issue is: should pupils wear school uniforms? His next step could be a risky one; he summarises the arguments he doesn't agree with. Why do you think this might be risky?

The development of the passage, though, is very logical, very precise. You are taken through a variety of ideas carefully, one at a time. Instead of bombarding you with lots of facts at the same time, the writer takes each one separately and examines it in detail. This is more convincing because:

a you are not being blinded by a rapid-fire set of ideas and

b you have the chance to look at each idea and study all that it might involve.

There are clear signpost words that help you to see the stage-by-stage structure of the argument: 'first', 'second', 'then', and 'the main argument'. Not only that, each stage is well supported by examples and explanations to allow you to develop a clearer picture. You can be in no doubt about which side of the argument the writer favours.

You should also notice that the passage is full of lists. The writer seems quite fond of lists. He uses these lists in several different ways: to create a fuller or wider picture that will allow you to visualise the meaning more easily; to show the extent of possibilities available; to make a definition more exact and less open to doubt or misinterpretation (you can't argue if there is a list of possible meanings, can you?); to show different stages or sides of one main idea (a list can break up a large idea into various smaller, more manageable ones).

Of course, some lists have more than one job to do; some do several of the above things at the same time. However, you should be aware of how they help to structure and support an argument.

It is also worth remembering that a list in a piece of argumentative writing is a most persuasive device: if one item on the list doesn't convince you, there are always several others to come along and try!

STUDY NOTES ON CREDIT LEVEL TEST 2
The Sweat Lodge

This passage is an example of writing about a personal experience. This means that something the writer feels was important or unusual has happened to him, and, because he has been affected by the experience, he wants to share his thoughts and feelings with you, the reader. In other words, the point of personal experience writing is to make you feel as if you were at an unusual, interesting or important event and were experiencing it in the same way as the writer.

In order to do this, the writer must do several things:

a First, he must catch your attention, to involve you in the experience. Can you think of several ways to catch attention? What about unexpected openings, descriptions of strange things, odd actions or unusual behaviour?

b Having caught your attention, the writer needs then to keep it. That will mean taking you through the experience in a logical, orderly fashion. If you are trying to understand how the writer thought and felt, it wouldn't help if you had no idea of what was actually happening. Therefore, the event must be described clearly and in the various stages in which it happened.

c The writer of personal experience wants you to feel as if you were there, at the event. That makes description very, very important. You must know *where* the event took place, *who* was there, *how* people behaved, *what* happened and *why* it was important, or unusual or exciting. The where? who? how? what? and why? should all be recorded in the passage and you, the reader, should be looking for such clues in a personal experience piece of writing.

d Last, but not of least importance, you should expect the writer to reveal a little (or a great deal) about what passed through his mind before, during and after the experience. After all, it is the writer's own way of looking at an event that makes it personal, that is, the experience of a single person, seen in a unique way and passed to you in an individual style.

Now, if you read over this particular piece of personal experience writing, look carefully to see how the writer does these things:

a How does he catch your attention? This must be in the opening paragraph. Is there anything unusual about it? Is the writer's behaviour different from normal behaviour?

b How does the writer keep your attention? The experience being described is a set pattern of events, a ritual, and the writer goes through each separate stage one after the other. This tells you about each part of the experience in the order in which it happened.

c What helps you to feel as though you were there? Well, you're told *where* the event happened, *who* was there, *how* they behaved, *what* actually took place, and *reasons* for the writer sharing the experience with you.

d What were the writer's thoughts and feelings? From the way events are described, and from comments the writer makes, you should be able to decide how he felt about the experience. In this case, do you think the writer is happy or unhappy to have had the experience? What words or phrases tell you this?

It is worth noting that some of the words use American spellings, eg smoldering (we write smouldering), and other words or phrases are special terms connected with the particular ritual, eg sweat lodge, medicine man. Can you imagine what these mean? What other words help you here?

Because the experience is a powerful one, the use of descriptive words is important to make the event come alive for the person reading about it. Look carefully at the adjectives used to describe the experience. Look at the wide range of feelings and how the experience goes *beyond* what the writer expected. Where does this begin to happen?

Lastly, what conclusion does the writer come to about the experience? How does he try to make sense of what happened to him?

STUDY NOTES ON CREDIT LEVEL TEST 3

Porphyria's Lover

This passage is quite different from any of the other ones used in this book. This is largely because you are dealing with a poem. To begin with, the language and style of poetry are different from prose. This is partly because the meanings have to be compressed into a definite pattern. The pattern is usually made using rhyme, fixed numbers of syllables in each line, and a set number of lines.

You will notice in this poem that there are sixty lines, that each word at the end of a line must rhyme with at least one other end-word, and that each line has eight syllables. The meaning is compressed into this rigid pattern.

Also, poetry often *suggests* rather than *states* a meaning. This means that you must look for hints and clues — and since this poem is about murder, it is very appropriate to be looking for clues.

The poem is a dramatic monologue, which simply means that it is being spoken by a single person in a dramatic situation. As you read the poem, you should be making up your mind who is speaking, where that person is, what has been done and why, and what sort of character the speaker is. The skill of the poet allows this information to be released only a little at a time, and only by hints and suggestions; so you'll have to think hard!

Like most poems, this one requires careful reading but your efforts will be rewarded! Points to look for include: the character and background of both Porphyria and the speaker; the setting; changes in mood of the speaker; a motive for murder; ways in which the language helps you piece together what is happening.

STUDY NOTES ON CREDIT LEVEL TEST 4

Great Expectations

This passage was taken from the opening chapter of Charles Dickens' novel *Great Expectations*. It describes a meeting between the main character, Pip, and a frightening man who is hiding in the graveyard.

Since it belongs to an opening chapter, the main business of this passage is to introduce to the reader the important characters. To create a character who will be interesting enough to make the reader want to read on, Dickens does several things:

1. He sets the opening in an interesting place—an old graveyard.

2. He describes a very unusual—and quite frightening—event.

3. He introduces a character that makes the reader want to know more—eg why is the man so wet and muddy? why has he a 'great iron' on his leg? where has he come from? will he persuade Pip to help him?

4. He places the main character, Pip, in such an awkward situation that the reader wants to find out whether Pip will be able to cope, and what Pip does to solve the difficulty.

You will also notice that Dickens creates his interesting characters in the ABC way. The ABC way simply means that you learn about a character

    A—from **A**ppearance (what does the man look like?)

    B—from **B**ehaviour (what sort of things does he do and say?)

And this gives you

    C—his **C**haracter (what he is like as a person)

In this passage, Dickens wants you to feel afraid—to feel the way Pip feels—because that will help you to identify with the main character, and see the world of the book through his eyes. But also, Dickens wants you to feel something more about the man—is he as bad as he appears? is there anything he says or does that is *not* frightening? are there hidden reasons for doing and saying what he does?

Also, look at the way Dickens says some things—clearly he is writing to make a big impression, so watch for the way characters speak (is it meant always to be realistic, and if not, why not?), for the use of repetition, for places where the author tries to avoid being so frightening as to put the reader off.

PS *Great Expectations* is a good read!

CHAPTER · FIVE ·
'THE WRITE STUFF'
How to Tackle Writing Assignments

You've heard it before. You'll hear it again. Exams are races against the clock. It's not the cleverest who always do best in exams. It's the students who make the best use of their time. That means you've not only to know *what* to do, but *how* long to take doing it.

Many students think that you can't study for the Writing paper in the Standard Grade English exam. How wrong can you be! There are skills you can practise, skills to be built up, tuned and sharpened that will make you fit and in good shape *before* the paper. Then, when it comes to the Writing paper, you'll be in peak condition — the right stuff!

The first stage of your writing training begins during your class work. You must try out all the different types of writing that Standard Grade English demands. Basically, there are *four* broad types:

1   Writing that *conveys information*. In other words, a piece of writing written mainly to tell the reader some important facts.
    Examples of type 1: a recipe; information about a hobby, or similar activity; instructions on how to do something or how to go somewhere.

2   Writing that *deploys ideas, expands, argues, evaluates*. In other words, a piece of writing that tells the reader what you think and believe about a subject, and what led you to think that way. This type of writing will also involve you in trying to persuade the reader to come round to your way of thinking.
    Examples of type 2: explaining your views on a controversial subject, eg answering the question 'Should school uniform be abolished?'; looking at the two sides of an argument and deciding with which one you agree; examining information and using it to make a case for a certain course of action.

3   Writing that *expresses feelings*, and *describes personal experience*. In other words, a piece of writing that allows the reader to share in the feelings of the writer, remember here — the feelings and experience *don't need to be your own* (although people always tend to write better about their own experiences and feelings).
    Examples of type 3: writing about an important or memorable event in your life (or the life of someone you are pretending to be); describing something that happened to you (or someone you are pretending to be) and explaining how you felt at the time, and perhaps how you feel about it now.

4   Writing that comes in a *specific literary form*. In other words, a piece of writing that is set out in a way that makes it the same as a particular type of literature.
    Examples of type 4: a newspaper article; a short story; a script; a piece of poetry.

'If there are *four* types to choose from,' you might say, 'why should I try all four? My Standard Grade Folio only needs *two* writing pieces!' That's true, but over the two years of your 'S' Grade course, you'll be writing more than two pieces. Why? Quite simply, because: a)   You want to have a choice as to what goes into your Folio, and b)   You want to be sure of which types of writing you're best at. If you only write two pieces, you'll have no choice, and no chance of sending the best you can do, since you'll never know whether the types of writing you didn't attempt might not be types you were really good at doing.

So, stage one is to try every type of writing to find your strengths (and, of course, your weaknesses). Only once you feel sure (and at least two tries at each type will be needed here) should you think about concentrating on three of the four.

The next stage is helpful not only for the exam, but for your Folio, too. The Folio needs two writing pieces: one of type 1 or type 2, and one of type 3 or type 4. That means that at home you should begin to practise type 1 or type 2 *and* type 3 or type 4; in other words narrow down to *two* types of writing. This should be done in fourth year.

How can you practise? Well, your practice should be a way of improving your writing *and*

That way, you not only improve writing skills, you also sharpen them up to examination speed and fitness.

THE WRITING ROUTINE: HOW TO IMPROVE YOUR SKILLS

The idea is this. You practise going through this routine until you know it so well, you do it quickly and almost automatically. You also can practise sections of the whole routine separately, to be sure of them and to feel at ease with them.

▶ STARTING POINT

You should know the following things from trying out all the different types of writing:
(i) The *two* types you think you are best at.
(ii) The type you feel most comfortable doing.

You need to know both of these things because the exam paper might not contain an example of your favourite type, or, at least, an example of it that suits you.

▶ STEP ONE

Narrow down your choice. In classwork, this won't normally apply, because in most cases your teacher will give you a single assignment. However, in exams, this is a very important step. You have already begun it before you enter the exam when you decide on the types of writing you are best at. Once you are in the exam, and the time is ticking away, it's important to pick out immediately the questions that involve your best types of writing. That way, you don't waste any precious minutes reading questions you will not be answering.

▶ STEP TWO

Decide on the demands of the question. You should have narrowed your choice down to two or three questions before moving on to this step. With each of the remaining two or three, you must make up your mind about what is actually involved. That means you need to know the following:
(i) What does the question want you to do?
(ii) What are you able to do within the question's limits?
(iii) How well do your abilities and the question's demands match up?

Let's examine each of these:
(i) What are the demands of the question, what does it want you to do? There are several ways the question can make demands. First, it can tell you in a general way what your piece of writing should be about: it can make *content demands*. If you don't listen to these demands, if you move away from them, or if you begin to write without really understanding the *content demands*, then your writing will not be *relevant*. No matter how clever and well written a piece of writing is, if it is not *relevant*, that is, if it doesn't stick to the point of the question, it will not do well. For this reason, being sure you know the *content demands* of a question is very important.

A question can also make demands about how you set out a piece of writing. These are *form demands*. For instance, a question may ask you to write about a subject, but in a particular way, such as asking you to write a magazine article. This means that you need to pay attention to *how* you set the writing out, as well as to what you put in it.

(ii) Once you know the demands of the question, you then have to think about what your abilities are. It may be that a question is on a subject you know something about. Its *content demands* are well suited to your abilities, because you have plenty of material you can write about. However, if the same question has difficult *form demands*, if it asks that you write the piece as a radio or TV script or a poem, and you know very little about writing such scripts or poems, it might not be a very suitable question for you to try. There could be another question which suits your abilities better.

(iii) The real test in deciding on which question is for you in an exam is by asking 'How well do the demands of the question match my abilities?' The question with the best match is the one to tackle.

▶ STEP THREE

Take charge of planning. You know the types of writing at which you are best. You've narrowed down the choice in your exam paper. You've made the best possible match between the demands of a question and your abilities.

Now that you've chosen a question, you must take charge of all the time left in the exam. You must be in control of the situation. Most mistakes are made when you are not in control, when you don't know what is going to happen. The only way to be in control of the situation, then, is to *plan* what should happen. Planning reduces the number of mistakes you are likely to make because planning puts you in control of what happens. Here is a list of common mistakes made in writing. Beside each mistake is an explanation of how planning (good, careful planning) reduces the chances of making these mistakes.

Common Mistake	**How Planning Helps**
The finished piece of writing is too short	There may be various reasons for this: it may be because you hadn't thought of enough ideas; or because you ran out of time due to thinking as you wrote (which means long pauses to gather your ideas together); or you didn't develop your ideas/situations enough. Whatever the reason, planning helps. A careful plan will not only include plenty of ideas but also explain how the ideas should develop. If you use planning time as thinking time, then when you write, you'll avoid long pauses to decide what to write next — all you do is look at the plan to tell you what to write about next.
It doesn't keep to the *demands* of the question	Very often when you have to think as you write, your ideas begin to wander away from the question. You begin to make connections between thoughts that take you further and further from the point. When you plan, you keep the question right in front of you. Indeed, part of your plan will contain your notes on the demands the question is making. The plan should also contain thoughts and ideas you want to mention, and it's easier to check in the plan whether each thought is relevant to the question than it is while you are involved in writing.
It is full of careless spelling and punctuation mistakes	Everyone is guilty of making these mistakes. Some people are not very good at spelling and punctuation. Often, however, such mistakes are the result of trying to do two things at the same time: working out what you're going to write about next *and* being careful about your spelling and punctuation. Planning what to write *before* you write it frees the mind to concentrate more on the basics of writing in paragraphs and sentences, and spelling and punctuating the piece correctly. In addition, a good plan will allow you a few minutes at the end of the exam for checking and correcting.
It is mixed up, its ideas are in no clear order	This usually happens when you tackle a large or a complicated subject. Ideas crowd in on your brain as you write and you put them down quickly before you forget them, until you've so much to say that what you said before has been forgotten! An essay with fewer ideas but a clearer order would get more marks. If only you'd sorted the subject into key areas, then broken these down into smaller, more manageable sections and decided on the best, most logical way of joining them all together *before* you started to write. If only you'd *planned*...
It takes too long to get to the main points	Really this is a form of failing to keep to the demands of the question. Unfortunately, it's fairly common. For the first page of an essay or an adventure story, you spend time telling the reader about the weather, or the clothes you wear, or what you had for breakfast instead of going straight to the point. Careful planning would make the beginning immediately interesting or exciting, to make the reader want to read on.

So you see, careful *planning* is crucial. Planning is the secret of control. You can remember this by the following rhyme:

Haven't a clue? At a loss?

BOSS could stand for **B**rainstorm, **O**rganise, **S**elect, and **S**equence.

These are the four stages of planning a good

▶**Brainstorm** This doesn't mean a hurricane in your head, so don't panic. Once you know the *content demands* and the *form demands* you should have some ideas about what to write. Your first job is to note down quickly all your thoughts on the subject of your essay, and on its layout, that come to you. These thoughts will include ideas for the beginning, the main event or central notion, and the ending; you can note interesting pieces of information on the subject, memories of your own experiences, clever phrases and maybe some technical terms you might use, as well as ways of presenting the material. Above all, you should try to come up with about half a dozen key ideas.

The point of this stage of planning is to gather quickly and widely as much material for your essay as possible. You don't worry yet about any order; note your ideas as they come into your mind. This is the art of brainstorming.

The more you practise brainstorming, the more material you should be able to gather for your writing because you'll find ideas come more quickly. If you can, find a friend to swap topics for brainstorming.

▶**Organise** As with any storm, a brainstorm can leave things looking chaotic. You've been so busy scribbling down ideas that they are all over the place. There should be lots of ideas noted here and there, but it's time now to tidy them up.

One of the neatest ways to organise ideas is to put them into boxes. So, if you can, divide a page into about six boxes. Give each box a heading: one box for the opening material of your essay, one for the ending and four (or perhaps a couple more) for the main part in the middle. Into each box you put notes you've made during brainstorming. Be careful that only notes on the same or a similar topic are put into the same box. Here is an example to give you an idea.

Imagine the subject was Cats. After your brainstorm you have lots of notes about different aspects of cats. You put similar notes into the same box. Thus a note like 'cats hunt at night' might go beside a note 'cats can see well in the dark'. These belong in the same box. Another set of notes on superstitions about cats, 'lucky black cat', 'cats have nine lives', 'witches' cats', would go into a different box. Gradually you hope to fill as many boxes as possible. As you do so, new, fresh ideas might come to you, so try to fit these in, too. Clever phrases, too, should be put into the boxes.

▶**Select** Of course, not all of the ideas that come to you will be brilliant. Some might be boring or unoriginal. Others, although quite clever, might not fit in with the rest. Clearly, you're going to have to select the best: ideas that are interesting, original and fit in with the other ideas you hope to include. There is little point in putting together ideas that contradict each other; they will only cancel each other out and, unless you are trying to show two sides of an argument, will confuse the reader who won't be sure you know what you're thinking.

At this stage, your motto should be: *Select the best, reject the rest*.

▶**Sequence** Once you've *organised* all the material that brainstorming produced, then *selected* the best of it, you must decide on the best order for dealing with it in your essay. You should do this sequencing *before* you begin writing.

Different orders of ideas or events suit different subjects. If you are describing how you would do something, it is best to begin at the beginning and work your way through the stages in the order they happen until you end with the final stage. On the other hand, if you are telling a story, you might choose to begin with the main character in a really tricky situation (this is always interesting) and use a technique called 'flashback'. Flashback makes the main character think back in time from the present tricky situation to the events which led up to the problem.

So, depending on how you want to write your essay, and on what your chosen subject is, you would sequence your ideas in a particular order.

To sum up, the Study-mate method for essay efficiency is as follows:
1. Find your favourite types of writing in your classwork.
2. In the exam, narrow down your choice quickly.
3. Decide on the demands of *content* and *form*.
4. Take charge of planning, remember *BOSS*: brainstorm, organise, select and sequence.
5. Write, write, write.
6. Read everything over to be sure it makes sense, and to correct careless mistakes.

Now it's time to look at some actual examples of Writing assignments.

CHAPTER·SIX
WRITING ASSIGNMENTS

WRITING ASSIGNMENT 1
CONVEYING INFORMATION

For an example of this type of writing you should take a look at the Reading passage used in Foundation Level Test 3. If you also look at the study notes on that passage in Chapter 4, you will find some ideas on how this kind of assignment should be written. Another place to look for help is General Level Test 1 and the study notes on that.

Assignment 'The Place Where I Live'

What you have to do. Imagine you have been asked to write a short piece for the Scottish Tourist Board. Your writing should tell tourists about life in the area where you live; what there is to see and what there is to do. Write a word-sketch of the place where you live.

WRITING ASSIGNMENT 2
ARGUING A CASE

For an example of this type of writing, you should take a look at the Reading passages used in General Level Test 4 and Credit Level Test 1. Also look at the study notes on these passages, that appear in Chapter 4, for some help on how to tackle this kind of assignment.

Assignment 'Rules'

First Look at the photograph below. It shows a rule book being thrown out of the window.

Next Take a moment to consider some of the rules that govern your lives. Are they necessary? Why do we have rules? Could they, or should they be changed?

What you have to do Write an argumentative essay in which you either agree or disagree that the rules we have are necessary and should not be changed.

WRITING ASSIGNMENT 3
DESCRIBING PERSONAL EXPERIENCE

For examples of this type of writing, you should take a look at the passages used in General Level Test 3 and Credit Level Test 2. The study notes on these passages (in Chapter 4) should also offer a few tips to help you in shaping your ideas on what to write and how to write it.

Assignment   'I Don't Think I'll Like It'

First   Look at the picture below. It has a very clear message.

Next   Consider to what sort of situations this message might apply. Think of times when you have used just such a phrase.

What you have to do   Write about a time when you were told that something was going to happen, or you were going to try something new, and you were worried that you wouldn't like it. Try to explain what your situation was, and concentrate on all your feelings. Remember to mention how everything turned out: was it as bad as you had imagined?

© Guiness Brewing GB 1988

WRITING ASSIGNMENT 4
WRITING A SHORT STORY

For an example of this type of writing, you should take a look at the Reading passage used in General Level Test 5. For ideas on how to create atmosphere and characters look at the passage in General Level Test 2, and the study notes on this passage in Chapter 4.

Assignment 'A Night In a Haunted Castle'

First Look at the photograph below. It shows a Scottish castle which is supposed to be haunted.

Next Imagine, for a moment, what the atmosphere in a haunted castle must be like: in the remote countryside; hardly a living soul for miles; darkness beginning to fall; and the castle the source of strange rumours and superstitions.

What you have to do Write a short story entitled 'A Night in a Haunted Castle'. Try to include interesting descriptions of the place and the atmosphere, as well as exciting events.

CHAPTER SEVEN
ANSWERS TO READING TESTS

ANSWERS TO FOUNDATION LEVEL INTRODUCTORY TEST
How the Cat Became

Because this is an introductory test, it is different from all the others. It aims to introduce you to the skills of active reading. The questions, then, don't try to cover the five main skills discussed in Chapter 2.

▶ SECTION 1

1 **a** pretty / fairly / all **b** retired / withdrew **c** nightmares **d** tucked / stuck **e** children / kids

1 mark for each correct answer. Maximum **5**.

2 (i) oddity (ii) start (iii) composing (iv) lounged (v) idly

1 mark for each correct answer. Maximum **5**.

▶ SECTION 2

1 paragraph d And try as he would
   paragraph e That night he went
   paragraph f Cat ducked back down
   paragraph g He tucked his violin
   paragraph h Other creatures
   paragraph i 'Cat's up to something,'

1 mark for each correct answer. Maximum **6**.

2 'That night': Cat is very tired / because the other animals pester him to work **2/0**
   'Cat ducked': Cat won't be persuaded / and has an idea **2/0**

▶ SECTION 3

1 Fiction / many possible reasons eg Cats or animals can't talk or don't behave that way **2/1/0**

2 **a** Cloud **2/0**
   b Clouds, like birds, move across the sky **2/0**

3 Cat is the only one unafraid of Man / He preferred Man to the complaints of the animals or Man had hunted the other animals, and killed them perhaps **2/1/0**

4 Man's eyes were wide **2/0**

5 Cat had long claws **2/0**

6 To make himself look confident / to show he wasn't scared **2/0**

7 (i) F
   (ii) F
   (iii) F
   (iv) T

   4 correct **2** marks
   3 correct **1** mark
   2/1/0 correct **0** marks **2/1/0**

8 He was a quick learner **2/0**

9 Cat's violin was his miaowing / his voice **2/0**

10 Anything sensible eg 'At last he's working.' 'I never thought he'd get a job' **2/0**

ANSWERS TO FOUNDATION LEVEL TEST 2
The Gooseberry

Question	Skill (see Chapter 2 for five types, a, b, c, d or e)	Answer	Marks
1	a	'The Runaway' / 'Noises at Night', or	

2	a	b/c	C because he had had a disturbed night	2/0
	b	b/c/e	Restless	2/0

3		b/c	Hobby: gardening / growing roses
			1 rising early
			2 locking doors
			3 making tea at breakfast at the weekend
			               3 correct **2** marks
			               2 correct **1** mark
			               1/0 correct **0** marks
				2/1/0

4	a	c	careful
			timid
			considerate
			               3 correct **2** marks
			               2 correct **1** mark
			               1/0 correct **0** marks
				2/1/0

	b	b	careful: Locks the door at night	2/0
			timid: Peered out gingerly / thought it was burglars / quickly closed the door	2/0
			considerate: Made tea for his wife	2/0
5	a	b	No	2/0
	b	b/c	Shot out (paragraph 4)	2/0
6	a	b	The back door is open	2/0
	b	b	Through a window	2/0
	c	b	There was a burglary nearby	2/0
7		c	He was scared / he wanted to protect her	2/0
8	a	b	Any *two* out of following three: 1 Stops 2 Puts hand to mouth 3 Says 'Ellen's gone!'	2/1/0
	b	c	She doesn't know all the facts / she is jumping to conclusions	2/1/0
	c	c/d/e	Ellen's gone, she's left the house / She's not in her bed, she's not there at the moment	2/1/0
9	a	c	He realises it's not burglars	2/0
	b	b	Ellen's gone out for a walk	2/0
	c	c	No / She did not look too convinced	2/1/0
	d	b	He gives her a cup of tea	2/0
10		c	It is addressed 'Mrs Hall' / instead of 'Mum'	2/1/0
11		a/b		

Note — You don't need to put the rooms in the same place as the diagram has them. You do need to mention the five rooms. **1** mark for each correct room marked.

5/0

```
           | back |
           | door |
  _____
 |         |          |              |
 | Kitchen | Bathroom |   Ellen's    |
 |         |          |   Bedroom    |
 |_____|_____|_____|
 |         |          |              |
 | Sitting |   Hall   | Rose and     |
 |  room   |          | Herbert's    |
 |         |          | Bedroom      |
 |_____|_____|_____|
                | front |
                | door  |
```

ANSWERS TO FOUNDATION LEVEL TEST 3

How to Complain

Question		Skill	Answer	Marks
1		a/b/c	1 Go back to the shop as soon as possible 2 Write to say it's faulty	2/1/0
2	a	b	The sellers	2/0
	b	b	Your contract is with them, not the manufacturers	2/0
3		b	Any *two* of the following: case / retailer / manufacturer / party	2/1/0
4		a/c/e	Heavy print: main ideas Normal print: explanation	2/1/0
5	a	b	A person in authority / manager	2/0
	b	b	To show you mean business	2/0
6	a	b	1 Manager not in 2 Manager is at a meeting	2/1/0
	b	b	1 Insist on seeing whoever is in charge 2 Make an appointment to come back	2/1/0
7		c	Claim	2/0
8	a	c/d	To avoid arguing / with someone you need to deal with	2/1/0
	b	b/c	Be polite but firm / give a business-like impression	2/1/0
9	a	c/d	Yes	2/0
	b	b/c	Remarkable	2/0

	c	b/c	D All your money back
			F Faulty goods mended
			G Chance to take a different item of same value
			H Replacement
			    4 correct **2** marks
			    3 correct **1** mark
			    2/1/0 correct **0** marks
				2/1/0

10		b	6	2/0
11		b/c/e	The seller owns the goods / it is not difficult, it explains itself	2/1/0
12		c	£205	2/0

13		b/d	If yes, explain why
			If no, explain why
			    Yes/No **1** mark
			    Explanation **1** mark
				2/1/0

14		b	(i) F (ii) O (iii) F 3 correct **2** marks	

ANSWERS TO FOUNDATION LEVEL TEST 4
Smith

Question	Skill	Answer	Marks
1	c	The grim hangmen's faces	2/0
2	b	He has to be scrubbed / washed	2/0
3	b	'No escape'	2/0
4	b	Twelve	2/0
5	c	Type of uniform	2/0
6 a	c	Somewhere in the attic	2/0
b	b	'Down to the scullery', paragraph 5	2/0
7 a	c	'Have you never seen a person take off his clothes before?' or similar	2/0
b	e	Because it makes Smith's speech more realistic.	2/0
8	c	Ready to laugh / amazement / disdain 3 correct **2** marks 2 correct **1** mark 1/0 correct **0** marks	2/1/0
9 a	b	He had never thrown any away	2/0
b	b/c	'Over-cured / slices of ham'	2/1/0
10 a	b	Livestock	2/0
b	c	No one took much care of him	2/0
11 a	c	Very nervous	2/0
b	c	Washed clean	2/0
12 a	b	1 One holds Smith 2 One scrubs him 3 One ladles out bugs 3 correct **2** marks 2 correct **1** mark 1/0 correct **0** marks	2/1/0
b	b/c	'faces grew red'	2/0
13 a	c/d	They were too dirty / to use again	2/1/0
b	c	He was quite sad	2/0
14	b	Thin / not at ease / dark-haired 3 correct **2** marks 2 correct **1** mark 1/0 correct **0** marks	2/1/0
15 a	a/c	About a hundred years ago	2/0
b	b	Footmen / iron tub / livery / breeches (any *one* for the marks)	2/0
16 a	a/b/c	Smith is given a bath	2/0
b	c	Anything sensible	2/0
17	a/d	Statement e	2/0
18 a	a/c	Fortunate	2/0
b	c/d	What was done helped or improved Smith	2/0

TOTAL 56

GRADES 56–42 — Grade 5 (Foundation Award)
41–22 — Grade 6 (Foundation Award)

ANSWERS TO GENERAL LEVEL TEST 1
Scotland's Heritage

Question	Skill	Answer	Marks
1	b	Gateway	2/0
2	e	To separate items in a list	2/0
3	b	C	2/0
4	b	To look after places / of historic importance	2/1/0
5	c	historic: P preserve: F Battle of Culloden: P throughout the centuries: P time honoured: P 4/5 correct **2** marks 3 correct **1** mark 2/1/0 correct **0** marks	2/1/0
6 a	c	C buildings that have an historic importance	2/0
b	b	Skara Brae	2/0
7	b	(ii) Paid for (iii) Free (iv) Free (v) Free (vi) Free 4/5 correct **2** marks 3 correct **1** mark 2/1/0 correct **0** marks	2/1/0
8	b/c	(i) £140 (ii) £110 (iii) £5 (iv) £20 3 correct **2** marks 2 correct **1** mark 1/0 correct **0** marks	2/1/0
9	e	Any *two* of: use of capital letters white on black background balanced phrase rhyme split by diamond top of the page	2/1/0
10	b/c	Someone who feels proud of his or her country / is patriotic / wants the best for Scotland	2/0
11	b/e	Any *two* of: soaring, peaceful or brooding	2/1/0
12	a/b	(i) gardening at Inverewe—growing palms *or* Brodick — rhododendrons *or* Threave — training head gardeners	2/0
		(ii) building at Culzean — viaduct *or* House of Dun — plasterwork	2/0
		(iii) conserving at Iona — beaches *or* Ben Lomond } paths Glencoe	2/0
13	a/d	(i) T (ii) T (iii) F 3 correct **2** marks	

Question	Skill	Answer	Marks
14	c/d	Restoring means returning to original condition Repairing means mending damage	2/0
15	c/e	'Unseen' here means that the restoration was done so skilfully that no one can tell just by looking at it when, or even if, it was done	2/0
16	b	National Trust for Scotland: 'All that we do, we do for you' / Historic Scotland: 'Become one of our friends'	2/1/0
17	b	National Trust for Scotland / 'Free admission to over 100 properties in Scotland + 300 in England' and 'free entry to 330 sites'	2/1/0
18	c	'For as little as £10 each year'	2/0
19 a	c/d/e	To give a sense of value for money / To emphasise you get a lot in return	2/0
b	b	A twelve-month period	2/0
20	a/b	Free admission and guided tours	2/0
21	a/d	Choosing either organisation is acceptable but a reason that relates to one pamphlet or the other is necessary for the marks	2/0

ANSWERS TO GENERAL LEVEL TEST 2

Dracula

Question	Skill	Answer	Marks
1	e	A diary or journal	2/0
2 a	c/b	C Late evening (**1** mark) and *either*: 'In the gloom' *or* 'I have not yet ... daylight' (**1** mark)	2/1/0
b	c	A castle (or similar) / because it has a courtyard and large arches	2/0
3 a	c	A type of carriage *or* vehicle	2/0
b	b/c	Pulled by horses *or* needs a driver	2/0
4 a	a/c	Nervous, worried, scared, doubtful	2/0

b	b/c/d	1 He is all alone
		2 He is far from home
		3 The place is dark and frightening
		    3 correct **2** marks
		    2 correct **1** mark
		    1/0 correct **0** marks
			2/1/0

c	c	They don't seem very friendly / and they are dark, gloomy	2/1/0
d	b	He pinches himself	2/0

5	a	b	In the Carpathians	2/0
	b	b	He is a solicitor, *not* a solicitor's clerk	2/0
	c	b	To tell him about buying a piece of property in London (Both 'property' and 'London' needed to gain the marks)	2/0
6	a	b/c	1 Old 2 Strong or powerful	2/1/0
	b	c	He was eager, keen to have Jonathan enter	2/0
7	a	b	It was very strong / his hand was very cold	2/1/0
	b	b	He appears to be old / the room was very warm	2/1/0
8	a	b	He thinks the driver and Dracula might be the same person	2/0
	b	b	The driver is very strong / he kept his face covered	2/1/0
9		b	Any *three* from bowed; carried luggage; had supper ready; had warm fire lit 3 correct **2** marks 2 correct **1** mark 1/0 correct **0** marks	2/1/0
10		c/b	Got rid of / dispersed / calmed (**1** mark) and 'my normal state' (**1** mark)	2/1/0
11		b/c	Differences (any four) 1 No moustache in picture 2 Not old 3 Ears not pointed 4 Eyebrows don't meet / not bushy 5 Hair not bushy / curly 4 correct **2** marks 3 correct **1** mark 2/1/0 correct **0** marks	2/1/0
			Similarities (any five) 1 Dressed in black 2 Domed forehead 3 Cruel mouth / sharp teeth 4 Very pale 5 Strong chin 6 Thin cheeks 5/4 correct **2** marks 3 correct **1** mark 2/1/0 correct **0** marks	2/1/0
12	a	b/c	He has a sickening effect on Jonathan / and causes him to shudder	2/1/0
	b	b/c	Because Dracula's breath was horrible	2/0
	c	b	Music	2/0
13		c/d	For this type of answer, you are expected to give an opinion and also to support it using the passage for evidence. Thus, a good answer here would be: Jonathan was quite worried / because Dracula seemed a very strange person	

14		c/e	(i) Dracula's strength *or* Jonathan's youth	2/0
			(ii) The rattle of the door being opened	2/0
			(iii) The chill of the night	2/0
			(iv) The strangeness of some of his behaviour (eg not eating) *or* his foul breath	2/0

ANSWERS TO GENERAL LEVEL TEST 3
Tartan Travels

Question		Skill	Answer	Marks
1	a	c	(i) undoubted / unquestionable / without doubt / certain / absolute	2/0
			(ii) habit / fashion	2/0
			(iii) compromise / allowance	2/0
			(iv) gather / summon up / collect	2/0
	b	b/c	(i) suicidal (paragraph 28)	
			(ii) witheringly (paragraph 30)	
			(iii) exuberance (paragraph 34)	
			(iv) ululating (paragraph 42)	
			4 correct **2** marks	
			2/3 correct **1** mark	
			1/0 correct **0** marks	2/1/0
2		b/c	1 'more poetic': sounded better	
			2 'more visual': allowed you to imagine it more easily / easier to picture	
			3 made writer seem less weak	
			3 correct **2** marks	
			2 correct **1** mark	
			1/0 correct **0** marks	2/1/0
3	a	c/e	To let you believe he is afraid of his wife *or* under her control *or* quite a weak character	2/0
	b	b	any examples of his fear of heights eg testing the cable	2/0
4	a	c/d	No / because there are no yaks, llamas or sherpas used in climbing in Europe	2/1/0
	b	c	1 He doesn't want to go to the summit	
			2 He hopes to put her off the idea	2/1/0
	c	c	No / she is 'blissfully ignoring' him *or* she insists on going, 'I want to go'	2/1/0
5	a	b/c	'gleam of battle'	2/0
	b	c/e	it is less insulting, less critical than the correct word / determined *or* firm *or* decided	2/1/0
6	a	b	He is afraid of heights	2/0
	b	b/c	She had never been with him in a high place / even his house had only one level	2/1/0
	c	c	1 without success	
			2 in a conceited or proud way	2/1/0

Question		Skill	Answer	Marks
7		c/e	Defeat usually causes unhappiness, and smiles usually show happiness / It is unusual for a happy sign to show something that normally brings unhappiness	2/1/0
8	a	b/c	The writer's fear	2/0
	b	c	Because there are no stewardesses or parachutes on cable-cars / and no parachute should be required	2/1/0
9		c/b	He doesn't like them or he thinks they are crazy, stupid, mad / he calls them 'suicidal' or he makes fun of them 'yodelling until a collision occurs' or he doesn't trust them ('Not a lot')	2/1/0
10	a	b	Downhill	2/0
	b	c	Downhill, in the downward direction ie from the top of Mont Blanc to the bottom / downhill, in the sense of becoming worse	2/1/0
11		b/c	Motherwell / even (paragraph 39)	2/1/0
12	a	a/c	It is about a Scots person travelling abroad / and the Italian tries to demonstrate the wearing of the kilt	2/1/0
	b	a/c	Because the Italian is not completely successful in pretending to wear the kilt, only partly successful	2/0

ANSWERS TO GENERAL LEVEL TEST 4
Elephants

Question		Skill	Answer	Marks
1	a	b/c	Having a memory like an elephant — good memory / having a memory title a sieve — poor memory	2/1/0
	b	c	Mythical	2/0
2	a	b	1 Elephants are biggest animal on land 2 They have been on Earth 60 million years longer than Man 3 There used to be over 300 types of elephant 4 There are only two types of elephant left Any 3 correct **2** marks 2 correct **1** mark 1/0 correct **0** marks	2/1/0
	b	c/b	Length of life or long-living / 'life-span documentation'	2/1/0
	c	c	They are false beliefs / they are untrue	2/0
	d	c	Paragraph 2 is accurate / true Paragraph 3 is superstition / false	2/0
3	a	c	C	2/0

Question		Skill	Answer	Marks
4	a	b	Because they can be captured / they can be successfully captured using the simplest of methods	2/1/0
	b	b/c	No / because they won't follow an elephant that manages to escape	2/1/0
	c	c/e	Because it proves the elephant didn't plan or intend to escape—it was accidental	2/0
5	a	b/c	1 Finding enough food to eat 2 Danger from the weather conditions 3 Danger from other animals 3 correct **3** marks 2 correct **2** marks 1/0 correct **1** mark	2/1/0
	b	b	Veterinary/medical care	2/0
6	a	b/c	Elephants could not live any longer in the wild	2/0
	b	b	They lose their teeth at sixty / then they cannot eat and must die	2/1/0
7		a/c	The last sentence of paragraph 3 introduces concepts of elephant intelligence or cunning, and long life / each of the remaining paragraphs deals with one of these topics in turn	2/1/0
8	a	a	That we have a lot of mistaken ideas about elephants	2/0
	b	d	Yes / because he used lots of evidence	2/1/0
9	a	d	Against	2/0
	b	b	Any piece of evidence that shows elephants are stupid eg Carrington's test, Indian trapping	2/0

ANSWERS TO GENERAL LEVEL TEST 5
The Lost Boy

Question		Skill	Answer	Marks
1	a	b	Orkney	2/0
	b	b	His Aunty Belle	2/0
	c	b/c	Ten 'Gone was my fat ... friend of the past ten winters' (paragraph 3)	2/1/0
	d	b/c	Angry, upset, unhappy etc. Anything that suggests a bad mood	2/0
2	a	b/c	1 He doesn't believe in Santa Claus any longer 2 The reindeer no longer exist 3 Santa's sledge has been shattered by Aunty Belle's news 4 The magic had left the hearth 3 correct **2** marks 2 correct **1** mark 1/0 correct **0** marks	2/1/0

	b	*b/c*	He thinks they are both cruel and deceitful (both needed for the marks)	**2/0**
	c	*c*	Deceitful because they tell lies about Santa / cruel because they have killed him: 'exiled my dear old friend, Santa Claus, to eternal oblivion' (paragraph 4)	**2/1/0**
	d	*b/c*	He thinks she is very bad tempered / Example: she boxed his ears at Hallowe'en Example: she would hit him if she knew he was outside on Christmas Eve (paragraph 21)	**2/1/0**
	e	*b/c*	She thinks she has done the right thing: 'piece of common sense' (paragraph 7)	**2/1/0**
3		*c/e*	'Bereaved' means left alone because someone has died / and, for the story-teller, Santa Claus seems dead	**2/1/0**
4		*b*	Time Evidence	
			(i) 'After tea' paragraph 2	**2/1/0**
			(ii) 'about half-past ten' paragraph 8	**2/1/0**
			(iii) 'I saw it . . . at eleven' paragraph 6	**2/1/0**
			(iv) 'that midnight' paragraph 21	**2/1/0**
5	a	*b*	His Aunty Belle's snoring	**2/0**
	b	*c*	Yes / because he says his clothes were cold so he must have been out of them for some time	**2/1/0**
6	a	*e*	They were sharp because the night was so cold it made them stand out clearly / they were like nails because they resembled the points of nails sticking out of the night sky	**2/1/0**
	b	*e*	The boy was drawn to the light of Jock's window / in the same way as a moth is drawn to the light of a flame	**2/1/0**
7		*b*	(i) a boy about the story-teller's own age (see paragraph 15) (ii) 'ingrained filth and hung cobwebs' (paragraph 14)	**2/1/0**
8	a	*b*	Three	**2/0**
	b	*c*	No, because he 'rejoiced in them' *or* he is delighted by them and treats them very carefully, as if they are precious (paragraph 15)	**2/0**
9		*c*	*pure* because it shows no signs of age or badness / that appear as black lines or furrows (paragraph 19) on old Jock's face	**2/1/0**
10		*c*	1 Because he was cold from being out on a bitter night 2 Because he was afraid his Aunty Belle might discover he had been out / might waken and catch him	**2/1/0**
11	a	*c*	To find out whether the boy was still	

b	d	Yes, because it had been so magical and now it was gone or everything was back to normal *or* No, because at least he knew there was still magic in Christmas and he couldn't expect the miracle to last forever	2/0
12	a/c	1 The 'Lost Boy' refers to the young boy in Jock's house, the boy Jock once had been but who is now lost in time 2 The 'Lost Boy' refers to the story-teller who is not the boy who once believed in Santa Claus *or* is a boy who had lost his belief in Santa Claus until he saw what happened in Jock's house	2/1/0
			TOTAL 52

GRADES 38–52   Grade 3 (General Award)
22–38   Grade 4 (General Award)
below 22 Foundation Award

ANSWERS TO CREDIT LEVEL TEST 1
The School Experience

Question	Skill	Answer	Marks
1 a	b/e	1 It introduces the subject of school uniforms 2 It summarises the arguments against wearing them	2/1/0
b	a/b/c	Paragraph 1 sets out the arguments against wearing uniform, and paragraphs 2–5 explain why these arguments are not valid / convincing	2/0
c	c	paragraphs 1–5 state the case for not wearing uniforms and show why this case is not a strong one. In paragraphs 6–10 the writer argues the case for wearing uniforms	2/0
2 a	c	Getting rid of school uniforms is a main idea / in the movement that wants pupils to have more control in schools	2/1/0
b	b	most (but not *all*) modern educationists	2/0
3 a	b/c	1 School uniforms reinforce or show the idea that pupils are inferior to teachers so that they keep pupils in a lower position	2/0
		2 School uniforms prevent pupils from being individual / original / unique in their choice of clothing. They suppress originality	2/0

			3 School uniforms are only affordable by wealthier families, and it means poorer pupils will stand out because they won't be wearing uniform like everyone else	2/0
	b	c/d	The rich and the poor	2/0
4	a	b	Every first year wears uniform	2/0
	b	c	It proves that it has nothing to do with being able to afford uniform / since not every person in first year is equally well-off, but every person does have a uniform	2/1/0
	c	b	1 It can treat all pupils equally 2 It can provide the chance for everyone to become involved in a wide range of activities	2/1/0
5	a	b	1 They wear team strips or scarves in order to show their support of a particular team at weekend matches 2 They wear the uniforms of a variety of organisations eg Scouts, Guides, BBs 3 They copy clothes worn by pop groups 4 They wear jeans which are broadly similar Any 3 correct **2** marks 2 correct **1** mark 1/0 correct **0** marks	2/1/0
	b	c	All of these involve deliberately dressing in the same way as others / and, therefore, not in a person's own, unique style — which, it is claimed, is what young people want	2/1/0
6	a	c	a mark or sign of shame or embarrassment	2/0
	b	b	'normal'	2/0
7	a	c/e	'sally forth' suggests showing no concern, ie they do not mind wearing uniforms	2/0
	b	b/c	1 authoritarian 2 subservience	2/1/0
	c	c/d	He does not think highly of them / because he is sarcastic about them ('perhaps pride' etc) or the idea that they are responsible for 'outlawing' something he is in favour of	2/1/0
8		b/c	1 Paragraph 6: School uniform makes the school a clearly visible part of the community, it links school and community 2 Paragraph 7: It prevents pupils drawing attention to themselves by wearing costly or strange dress 3 Paragraph 8: It helps to reinforce a smart and effective attitude to work	

		spectacle / adds colour to important occasions and makes them more memorable 5 Paragraph 10: It supports and demonstrates the bond between pupils, and offers them evidence of companionship **2** marks for each correct answer. Maximum **6**	
9	b/c	Any *two* of the following: Paragraph 1: 'pupil power' — to show a technical term used in the abolitionists' policy Paragraph 2: 'trendy' — to show a colloquial / slang expression, not one used in formal argument 'no mean city' — a quotation from the Bible Paragraph 7: 'show off' — to show a colloquial / slang phrase. **1** mark for examples chosen; **1** mark for correct explanation	**2/1/0**
10	d/e	Either yes or no is possible here. What is important is that you use your reading to explain your response. If yes, you would say something about how clearly or how well illustrated the argument was. If no, you would suggest points and reasons for your disagreement — eg by showing flaws in the writer's argument. **1** mark for yes / no; **1** mark for a reason	**2/1/0**

ANSWERS TO CREDIT LEVEL TEST 2

The Sweat Lodge

Question	Skill	Answer	Marks
1 a	c	Use of grandfathers, plural, to mean ancestors	**2/0**
b	b/c	Begged, beseeched, pleaded with (**0** marks for 'asked', not strong enough)	**2/0**
c	c/e	They come in pairs **1** mark All suggest not able to talk properly / not in full control **1** mark	**2/1/0**
d	c	He was very emotional	**2/0**
e	b	'even'	**2/0**
2 a	c/d/e	Captures attention / makes you want to know why or what is going on	**2/1/0**
b	b	1 One of most fascinating / interesting rituals **1** mark	

			2 He didn't know what it would involve	
			1 mark	2/1/0
	c	b/c/d	Yes / 'thus far'	2/1/0
3	a	c/e	It makes the event seem as if it is happening *now* / and that involves the reader more	2/1/0
	b	b	To prevent writer building up expectations *or* to allow writer to experience the sweat without knowing what was going to happen	2/0
	c	a/b	1 buy cloth and tobacco 2 wrap tobacco in cloth 3 take off their clothes 3 correct **2** marks 2 correct **1** mark 1/0 correct **0** marks	2/1/0
4		a/b	(i) Shape of floor: circular	2/0
			(ii) Height of lodge: 4ft	2/0
			(iii) Breadth: 10ft	2/0
			(iv) Decoration: buffalo skulls	2/0
			(v) Material of frame: wood / poplar	2/1/0
			(vi) Material of covering: animal hide	2/0
			(vii) Number of windows: none	2/0
			(viii) Number of doors: one	2/0
			(ix) Contents: Pit of hot stones / in centre of floor	2/1/0
5	a	b/c	Comfortable because it's warm / outside it is bitterly cold	2/1/0
	b	b/c	Uncomfortable because his legs are cramped / there's not much room inside	2/1/0
6		b	1 *Each one* waving burning sweet grass 2 *Each one* smoking peace pipe 3 *Each one* drinking / sprinkling water 3 correct **2** marks 2 correct **1** mark 1/0 correct **0** marks	2/1/0
7	a	b	The hot stones in the pit glow dimly	2/0
	b	c/e	'Feverishly' suggests very high temperature / these rocks have been heated all day	2/1/0
	c	c/b	Nervous *or* anxious *or* worried / and 'eerily' *or* 'startles'	2/1/0
8	a	b/c	1 Change in the level of noise 1 mark 2 Change in the degree of discomfort 1 mark	2/1/0
	b	b	Noise: others join in / softly *at first* 1 mark Discomfort: now 'drenched in perspiration' / now breathe with difficulty / 'distracting me from my discomfort' /	

	c	c/d	The sweat doesn't only have an effect on people with no experience (like the writer) / it is affecting everyone. All in it together	2/1/0
9	a	b	Everyone moaning, groaning and swaying in greater need	2/0
			The end of the first sweat / opening the door	2/0
	b	b/c	'soon'	2/0
			'until'	2/0
10		a/c/e	The duration of the sweats seems long and hard (mentioned in paragraphs 8 and 10) / the break between sweats (paragraph 9) seems short	2/1/0
11	a	b	The sweat can prove too much for some people / and it is not wise, in that case, to remain	2/1/0
	b	c/d	Although in some ways he would like to be able to leave / he doesn't want to let others feel he cannot finish it. He wants to see it through to the end	2/1/0
12	a	b/c	'Perhaps I am beginning to hallucinate'	2/0
	b	b	Ritual	2/0
	c	c	The sweat is no longer just a series of ceremonies that are carried out to follow tradition (ie not a ritual any more) / It is a genuine experience the author goes through. He's not going through the motions, he really *feels* the importance of the event.	2/1/0
13	a	b/c	The medicine man: No two people see the sweat in the same way / but it is not always possible to say how each one experiences it	2/1/0
			The writer: The sweat can only be lived through / and it is not possible to convey its impact in words	2/1/0
	b	b/c	Some type of scientist / 'our scientific comprehension' *or* 'words, logic, science might not be enough'	2/1/0
14		a/c/e	A host usually makes people feel welcome and looks after them. / This host put the writer through a difficult / painful experience	2/1/0

ANSWERS TO CREDIT LEVEL TEST 3

Porphyria's Lover

Question	Skill	Answer	Marks
Section One			
1 a	c/e	As a person / in a temper	2/1/0

	b	b/c	As a person: 'awake' / In a temper: 'sullen' or 'spite' or 'vex'	2/1/0
2	a	b/c	She moves smoothly, suggesting calmness (from 'glided') compared with the speaker's troubled nature (from 'heart fit to break') NB *Contrast* means you mention *both* sides: Porphyria / speaker	2/0
	b	c/d/e	1 It is cheerless because it has no fire in it 2 It is associated with the unhappiness of the speaker	2/1/0
3	a	a/b/c	The speaker is passive and silent, he only responds by being made to do something, or by guidance	2/0
	b	c	He is upset / not in a good mood / unhappy with her	2/0
	c	b	He won't talk, 'No voice replied' (line 15) / He needs to be made to do things, 'made my cheek lie there' (line 19)	2/1/0
4	a	b	A conflict between her pride and her passion / love	2/0
	b	a/b/c	No / because she comes to see him despite the weather *and/or* despite being expected at a feast elsewhere (line 27)	2/1/0
	c	b	Her pride	2/0
5	a	c	No	2/0
	b	b/c	Any *two* of the following: 1 He was sitting with heart fit to break (line 5) 2 The weather was terrible (lines 1–4) 3 Porphyria should have been at a feast (line 27)	2/1/0
6		c/d	Either *one* of the following: 1 Because she is of a higher social rank (he lives in a cottage / she goes to feasts, she has 'vainer ties') 2 She is not willing or able to leave this background ('too weak .. vainer ties dissever') *and / or* he is not sure she loves him enough ('for all her heart's endeavour')	2/1/0

Section Two

1		c/d	Because if you know he feels happy and proud then you are expected to realise that he murdered her for a good reason, not because the love was one-sided. She is murdered because she loves him, not because she doesn't love him	2/0
2	a	b	He is finally sure that Porphyria loves him	2/0
	b	b/c	Surprise / uncertainty *or* confusion *or*	2/1/0

3	a	c/e	*Either* that the speaker is very possessive *or jealous or* that the speaker is experiencing *intense* feeling	2/0
	b	c/e	By showing the strength of the speaker's feelings it might suggest that he is capable of violence, especially since they are feelings of possessiveness / jealousy	2/0
4	a	c/e	The simple language reflects the over-simplicity of the speaker's thinking / it suggests insanity in wanting to murder someone you love *or* simple language makes the murder more of a surprise because you don't expect it and makes the murder seem more horrible because it is described in such a matter-of-fact way	2/1/0

	b	b/c	1 He opens her eyes
			2 Unwinds the hair from her neck
			3 Kisses her cheek
			4 Places her head on his shoulder
			    4 correct **2** marks
			    3 correct **1** mark
			    2/1 correct **0** marks
				2/1/0

	c	d	You may feel that these actions show that he does not realise properly what he has done *or* you may think that these show how much he loves her and they help you to sympathise with the speaker (The important thing is that you give a full explanation)	2/0
5	a	b	Change from past tense to present tense	2/0
	b	c/d/e	Until the present tense is used, you can imagine yourself anywhere eg in the prison listening to the murderer admit his crime, in the police station or court-room. Once the present tense is used, you are beside the murderer in his cottage and Porphyria is lying dead in his arms as he speaks: 'thus we sit together *now*'	2/0

Section Three

1		a/c/e	The violence of the weather hints at the later violence of the speaker / the storm outside the cottage is similar to the storm in the speaker's heart and mind	2/0
2		a/c	He kills her because it is the only way to preserve the love she feels: 'that moment she was mine' / If he had not killed her, she was not strong enough in his opinion, to break free of her other connections 'too weak ... vainer ties'	2/1/0
3	a	b	The alternative is the speaker himself, and his love	2/0
	b	b/c	'instead' (line 55)	2/0

96

c	c	The connections and duties Porphyria had with people other than the speaker	2/0
d	b	'Vainer ties' (line 24)	2/0
e	c/d	'Vainer ties' has more of the idea that Porphyria felt connected, and owed duties, to people other than the speaker / 'All it scorned' suggests that she didn't care, in the speaker's opinion, about anything other than him	2/1/0
4	a/d	If yes, evidence is that he has not been judged by God: 'still God has not said a word' (line 60) If no, evidence is that he expects judgement (line 60) *or* that he contradicts himself in the way he describes what he believes are Porphyria's feelings about those people other than himself In questions like this you may answer either way: what is important is that you back up your answer with evidence from the text (this shows you have read and understood it!)	2/1/0

ANSWERS TO CREDIT LEVEL TEST 4
Great Expectations

Question	Skill	Answer	Marks

1 a	b	1 His voice
		2 The fright of his sudden appearance
		3 The chains on his leg
		4 The roughness of his appearance
		5 His threats
		    Any 3 correct **2** marks
		    2 correct **1** mark
		    1/0 correct **0** marks
			2/1/0

b	c	Pity / sorry for him / because he has 'broken shoes', 'lamed', 'cut', 'shivered' etc.	2/1/0
c	b	Any *two* of the following: 1 'Tell *us* your name' 2 'Give it mouth' 3 'Hold your noise'	2/1/0
d	d	It helps to emphasise his roughness *or* It makes him a more terrifying character *or* It makes him more realistic	2/0
2 a	c	About ten	2/0

b	b/c	1 'You little devil' (paragraph 1)
		2 He could be turned upside down easily (paragraph 10)
		3 'You young dog' (paragraph 11)
		    3 correct **2** marks
		    2 correct **1** mark	

3	a	*c*	That she had arrived in the graveyard / that she was coming to collect Pip	2/0
	b	*b*	He starts, jumps / he made to run away, he took fright	2/1/0
	c	*c*	He was scared / and on the run *or* He was afraid / because he was trying to escape or avoid being caught	2/1/0
	d	*b*	He had a great iron on his leg—like a convict *or* he wore grey uniform of prison	2/0
	e	*c/b*	He is quoting from the tombstone / use of inverted commas or similar quotation for father's grave: 'late of this parish'	2/1/0
4	a	*b/c*	Joe is Pip's brother-in-law	2/0
	b	*c*	A blacksmith might help to remove the iron from the man's leg / because he has instruments for cutting iron eg a file	2/1/0
5	a	*c*	Food	2/0
	b	*c/d*	See paragraph 34 'I would get him the file ... broken bits of food ...'	2/0
6	a	*c/e*	If effective, reason must be to do with the humour of maintaining politeness under pressure / If not effective, reason must be to do with the unrealistic speech of a young boy in that situation	2/1/0
	b	*c/d/e*	To make the situation slightly humorous / To keep our sympathy partly with the man	2/1/0
7	a	*b*	Any *two* of the following (need *two*): 1 That young man ... That young man 2 A boy may lock his door, may be ... 3 Softly creep and creep	2/0
	b	*d/e*	1 Repetition for emphasis 2 Repetition to show full range of possibilities 3 Repetition to suggest slow / stealthy movement	2/1/0
8	a	*c*	The threat of the young man is the way the man will force Pip to return / because he must let Pip go to fetch the file and the food	2/1/0
	b	*c/d*	Yes or no is acceptable but to get marks, a reason is necessary. A 'yes' reason might be that the convict had an accomplice to help him escape. A 'no' reason might be that there is no evidence of his presence.	2/1/0
9		*a*	Anything that covers the whole passage eg 'The Boy and the Prisoner'	2/0

ANSWERS TO CREDIT LEVEL TEST 5
The Mouse

Question		Skill	Answer	Marks
1	a	b/c	1 confines 2 solicitude 3 screened 　　　　　　　　　3 correct **2** marks 　　　　　　　　　2 correct **1** mark 　　　　　　　　　1/0 correct **0** marks	2/1/0
	b	b/c	She thought life was too rough	2/0
	c	c	Sheltered / protected or similar	2/0
2		c/e	It shows that what seems simple to normal people / is difficult to Theoderic	2/1/0
3	a	c	They would annoy him	2/0
	b	c	He was easily upset	2/0
4		b	Things that cause Theoderic to be annoyed or to feel ruffled	2/0
5	a	b/c	The organisation / of running a house	2/1/0
	b	b	Any *four* from the following: 1 carriage not ordered properly 2 the handyman unavailable when needed 3 out-house badly lit 4 infested with mice 5 Theoderic had to harness pony himself **2** marks for each correct answer. Maximum **8**	
6		c/e	'Petty annoyances' is a description from the normal point of view / 'disaster' changes to Theoderic's point of view	2/1/0
7		c	He is too timid to say anything	2/0
8	a	c	Destroy / the species *or* kill / *all* mice (You must say *all* or *species* for full marks)	2/1/0
	b	c/e	It is a euphemism / how Theoderic would say it to avoid mentioning anything nasty	2/0
9		a/c	1 He is easily disturbed 2 He is very timid 3 He doesn't know much about the real world 　　　　　　　　　3 correct **2** marks 　　　　　　　　　2 correct **1** mark 　　　　　　　　　1/0 correct **0** marks	2/1/0
10		b/c	He thought he smelled badly / He thought he looked untidy, with straw on	

11		b	1 There was a lady in the carriage 2 He could not leave the carriage 3 There were no stops 3 correct **2** marks 2 correct **1** mark 1/0 correct **0** marks	2/1/0
12		b/c	1 He thought there was more than one mouse in his clothes 2 He blushed at the thought of removing his outer clothes in front of a lady	2/1/0
13		c	He didn't want anyone to see his annoyance, he was so timid	2/0
14	a	c/e	That Theoderic is over-imaginative because he can regard himself as a place where mice can seek shelter	2/0
	b	c	Part of the metaphor of housing / property used to describe Theoderic	2/0
15	a	a/c	Late 1800s, early 1900s	2/0
	b	b/c	Use of pony and cart means before widespread use of cars / old fashioned or Victorian name, Theoderic	2/1/0
16		a	The Mouse refers to the actual mouse in Theoderic's clothes / The Mouse refers to Theoderic's personality	2/1/0
17		a/d	Anything sensible, not out of character	2/0
				TOTAL 54

GRADES 42–54 Grade 1 (Credit Award)
          28–41 Grade 2 (Credit Award)
          Below 28 General Award

ACKNOWLEDGEMENTS

The Author and Publisher would like to thank the following for permission to reproduce copyright material, some of which has been adapted for use in this book.

How the Cat Became
Reprinted by permission of Faber and Faber Ltd from *How the Whale Became* by Ted Hughes

The Gooseberry
Reprinted by permission of Hamish Hamilton Ltd from *The Gooseberry* by Joan Lingard (Hamish Hamilton,1978) © Joan Lingard 1978

How to Complain
Reprinted by permission of The Association for Consumer Research

Smith
Reprinted by permission of Penguin Books Ltd from *Smith* by Leon Garfield (Constable, 1967)
© Leon Garfield 1967

Scotland's Heritage
Reproduced by permission of Historic Scotland (*page* 27) and The National Trust for Scotland (*pages* 28–29)

Elephants
Reprinted by permission of Wadsworth Inc. from *Psychology* by Guy R. Lefrançois © 1980. All rights reserved.

The Lost Boy
Reprinted by permission of Chatto and Windus Ltd from *Andrina and other Stories* by George Mackay Brown

The School Experience
Reprinted by permission of Mr Wm Scobbie from *The School Experience* by James K. Scobbie

The Sweat Lodge
Reprinted by permission of Wadsworth Inc. from *Psychology* by Guy R. Lefrançois © 1980. All rights reserved.

The Author and Publisher would also like to thank the following for supplying photographs and other illustrative material and for giving their permission to reproduce these in this book.

Abbott Mead Vickers SMS Ltd   *page 76*
Guiness Brewing GB   *page 77*
Historic Scotland   *pages 27*
National Trust for Scotland   *pages 28–29, 78*

Copyright © by Universal Pictures, a Division of Universal City Studies, Inc. Courtesy of MCA Publishing Rights, a Division of MCA Inc.   *page 33*
Additional illustrations by **Dorothy Hamilton**